MEDICAL TREATMENT AND THE LAW

THE PROTECTION OF ADULTS AND MINORS IN THE FAMILY DIVISION

MEDICAL TREATMENT AND THE LAW

THE PROTECTION OF ADULTS AND MINORS IN THE FAMILY DIVISION

Richard S Harper MA(Oxon)

A District Judge of the Principal Registry of the Family Division

 **Family Law**

1999

Published by Family Law
a publishing imprint of
Jordan Publishing Limited
21 St Thomas Street, Bristol BS1 6JS

British Library Cataloguing-in-Publication Data
A catalogue record for this book is available from the British Library.

ISBN 0 85308 550 1

Typeset by Mendip Communications Ltd, Frome, Somerset
Printed by MPG Books Ltd, Bodmin, Cornwall

Foreword

A new statutory framework was introduced by the Mental Health Act 1959 to manage those suffering from permanent mental disability, and the entire structure previously in place was swept away. In recent years, the High Court has grappled with the wider problems of mental incapacity, not covered by the current mental health legislation. The House of Lords, in a series of decisions, has laid down guidelines for the courts and the medical profession. This admirable new work comprehensively reviews the present state of the law in a rapidly developing and increasingly complex area. Under the general heading of protection, the book deals with the case-law on capacity to consent to and, often more important, to refuse treatment, the position of those permanently unable to give consent and those temporarily incapable. It also covers the position of children, both those on behalf of whom irreversible and life-or-death decisions have to be made and those who may be of an age to make decisions themselves, including whether to undergo medical assessments. The case on mercy killings and medical treatment other than for medical reasons, such as sterilisation, in-vitro fertilisation, blood tests and the position of the unborn child are also included.

This book is a valuable addition to the library of judges and lawyers who may find themselves dealing with these legal and medical issues coming with greater frequency to the High Court, Family Division, and to the appellate courts. It is also a most helpful guide to the medical profession and hospital trusts as well as to local authorities, and all those engaged in the difficult and worrying task of advising on or making decisions for those who are for one reason or another unable to decide for themselves.

DAME ELIZABETH BUTLER-SLOSS
February 1999

Preface

This book is intended as an introduction to a complex and developing area of the law.

Many factors have contributed to the developments in the law, including advanced medical treatment now available, the number of elderly persons now living longer and the increasing desire among patients to question medical decisions. Whatever the background reasons, the courts are having to pick their way through the minefield of issues arising in medical treatment cases, particularly in relation to questions of competency, incompetency and consent.

The issues often involve principles of law, ethics and medical practice and the process has not been helped by the jurisdictional differences in the position of minors and adults. As this book shows, whilst the parens patriae jurisdiction remains to this day in relation to minors, there is no such jurisdiction in relation to adults who are, or may be, incompetent. The Law Commission in its Report on Mental Incapacity (No 231) recommended a statutory formula to encompass many of the areas raised in this book. The present Government has responded by issuing its Green Paper entitled 'Who Decides?'. Whether, and to what extent, legislation is passed remains to be seen. Further, the Human Rights Act 1998, which has now received Royal Assent, will, no doubt, in due course, impinge on this area of the law as well as many others.

What is intended in this book is to provide practical guidance and assistance as to the approach taken by the courts on all the varying issues raised in relation to medical treatment and the law, the thread of which throughout is the question of 'consent'.

The substance of this book may, accordingly, be of assistance not only to the legal profession but also to those working within the field of medicine or any other area concerned with the welfare of such adults or minors as are considered within.

It is to be noted that the details of leading cases which interlink a number of important issues are referred to at several points in the book. This will enable practitioners to consider those details in the context of the particular subject or chapter they wish to investigate.

I am most grateful to Dame Elizabeth Butler-Sloss for writing the Foreword to the book and to Magdalen College Oxford for permitting me to use its facilities for research. I wish to thank the following persons who, in differing ways, assisted with the preparation of the book: Fay Baker (barrister), Igor Vertkin, Martin West

(Jordans), Marva Sloley, District Judge Robert Conn, Michael Hinchliffe (Official Solicitor's Office) and Professor Robert Tyce. My final and most important thanks are to my family for their unfailing support and assistance.

RICHARD S HARPER
London
March 1999

Contents

Table of Cases

All references are to paragraph numbers, apart from those prefixed A which refer to Part III, Appended Materials

Table of Statutes

All references are to paragraph numbers, apart from those prefixed A which refer to Part III, Appended Materials

Table of Statutory Instruments and International Legislation

All references are to paragraph numbers, apart from those prefixed A which refer to Part III, Appended Materials

Table of Abbreviations

BMA   British Medical Association
CPR   cardio-pulmonary resuscitation
CT   computed tomography
CVS   continuing vegetative state
DNR   do-not-resuscitate
ECT   electro-convulsive therapy
FPR 1991   Family Proceedings Rules 1991
GID   Gender Identity Dysphoria
HFEA   Human Fertilisation and Embryology Authority
MRI   magnetic resonance imaging
NHS   National Health Service
PET   positron emission tomography
PVS   permanent vegetative state
RCN   Royal College of Nursing
RSC   Rules of the Supreme Court 1965

Part I

GENERAL PRINCIPLES IN RELATION TO MEDICAL TREATMENT AND THE LAW

Chapter 1

MEDICAL TREATMENT AND CONSENT

1.1   THE MEANING OF 'CONSENT'

'Consent' is the voluntary and continuing permission of a patient to receive a particular medical treatment, based on an adequate knowledge of the purpose, nature, likely effects and risks of that treatment including the likelihood of its success and any alternatives to it. Permission given under any unfair or undue pressure is not a true 'consent'.

1.2   THE PURPOSE OF CONSENT TO TREATMENT

There are two purposes of seeking consent from a patient, whether that patient is an adult or a child, or from someone with authority to give that consent on behalf of the patient. One purpose is legal and the other is clinical.

The legal purpose of consent is to provide those concerned in the treatment with a defence to a criminal charge of assault or battery or a civil claim for damages for trespass to the person. It does not, however, provide them with any defence to a claim that they negligently advised a particular treatment or negligently carried it out.

The clinical purpose of consent is that the co-operation and confidence of the patient in the efficiency of the treatment is often a major factor in the success of the treatment. Failure to obtain consent can not only disadvantage the patient and the medical staff, but can also make it more difficult to administer the treatment which can be the case if consent is given on behalf of, rather than by, the patient himself. However, in the case of young children, knowledge of the fact that the parent has consented may help.

This dual purpose of consent to medical treatment is set out in the case of in *Re W (A Minor) (Consent to Medical Treatment)* [1993] 1 FLR 1.

1.3   ADULTS OF SOUND MIND, MINORS AND THOSE SUBJECT TO INCAPACITATING MENTAL ILLNESS

The law respects the right of adults of sound mind to physical autonomy. Generally speaking, no one is entitled to touch, examine or operate upon such persons without their consent, express or implied. It is up to such persons to give or withhold consent as they wish, for reasons good or bad.

This simple rule cannot be applied in cases of minors and those subject to serious mental illness, because they may be unable to form or express any, or any reliable, judgment of where their best interests lie: *Re S (Hospital Patient: Court's Jurisdiction)* [1995] 1 FLR 1075, CA at 1087.

1.3.1 Adults of sound mind

The requirement of consent before medical treatment
At common law, a doctor cannot lawfully operate on adult patients of sound mind, or give them any other treatment involving the application of physical force, however slight, without their consent: in *Re F (Sterilisation: Mental Patient)* [1990] 2 AC 1, HL at 55.

If a doctor does operate on such patients or give them other treatment without their consent, that doctor is liable to be subject to a criminal charge of assault or an action in tort of trespass to the person.

The autonomy of the individual and the principle of self-determination
If an adult of sound mind refuses consent to medical treatment, the doctor must abide by his patient's decision. This is called the 'principle of autonomy of the patient'. It is described by Lord Goff in his article entitled 'A Matter of Life and Death' (1995) 3 *Medical Law Review* Spring.

The extent of the principle of autonomy and self-determination is such that every adult has the right and capacity to decide whether or not he will accept medical treatment, even if a refusal may risk permanent injury to his health or even lead to premature death. Furthermore, it does not matter whether the reasons for the refusal are rational or irrational, unknown or even non-existent: *Re T (An Adult) (Consent to Medical Treatment)* [1992] 2 FLR 458, CA at 473.

The right of self-determination was considered in *Airedale NHS Trust v Bland* [1993] AC 789, per Lord Goff at 864:

> '... it is established that the principle of self-determination requires that respect must be given to the wishes of the patient, so that if an adult patient of sound mind refuses, however unreasonably, to consent to treatment or care by which his life would or might be prolonged, the doctors responsible for his care must give effect to his wishes, even though they do not consider it to be in his best interests to do so ... To this extent, the principle of the sanctity of human life must yield to the principle of self-determination ... and, for present purposes perhaps more important, the doctor's duty to act in the best interests of his patient must likewise be qualified.'

It is necessary to emphasise that there are occasions when an individual lacks the capacity to make decisions about whether or not to consent to treatment. The presumption of capacity to decide is rebuttable, yet often it may be difficult for medical practitioners to adjudge whether an adult has or has not the requisite capacity to decide.

Breaching the principles of self-determination and the autonomy of the individual

The principles of self-determination and the autonomy of the individual and the effects of breaching them were reinforced in the case of *St George's Healthcare NHS Trust v S; R v Collins and Others ex parte S* [1998] 2 FLR 728, CA. On seeking to register as a new patient at a local NHS practice, S, who was 36 weeks pregnant, was found to be suffering from pre-eclampsia and was advised by the doctor that she needed urgent attention and admission to hospital for an induced delivery and that without such treatment her health and life and the life of her baby were in danger. S fully understood the potential risks but rejected the advice as she wanted her baby to be born naturally. She was seen by a social worker approved under the Mental Health Act 1983 and two doctors. They repeated the advice but she again refused to accept it. On the social worker's application, S was admitted to a mental hospital against her will for assessment under s 2 of the 1983 Act. A few hours later, again against her will, she was transferred to another hospital where she adamantly refused to consent to treatment and recorded her refusal in writing. She also then consulted solicitors. In view of her continuing refusal to consent to treatment, an ex parte application was made to the court without the issue of a summons and without the judge being informed either that S had instructed solicitors or that she and her solicitors were ignorant of the proceedings. The judge granted a declaration dispensing with S's consent to treatment and later the same evening her baby was born by Caesarean section. A few days later, S was returned to the mental hospital. Two days after that, her detention under s 2 of the 1983 Act was terminated and she immediately discharged herself from the hospital. She appealed the grant of the declaration dispensing with her consent to treatment and applied for a judicial review of her admission and detention in the mental hospital, her transfer, detention and treatment in the second hospital and her return to the mental hospital.

In relation to the autonomy of the patient involved and breaching such autonomy, the findings of the Court of Appeal in S's favour amounted to the following:

(1) even when his or her own life depends on receiving medical treatment, an adult of sound mind is entitled to refuse it;
(2) whilst pregnancy increases the personal responsibilities of a woman, it does not diminish her entitlement to decide whether or not to undergo medical treatment;
(3) an unborn child is not a separate person from its mother and its need for medical assistance does not prevail over her rights;
(4) a woman is entitled not to be forced to submit to an invasion of her body against her will, whether her own life or that of her unborn child depends on it;

(5)   her right is not reduced or diminished merely because her decision to exercise it may appear morally repugnant;

(6)   the declaration in the case granted at first instance involved the removal of the baby from within the body of her mother under physical compulsion. Unless lawfully justified, this constituted an infringement of the mother's autonomy. Of themselves, the perceived needs of the foetus did not provide the necessary justification;

(7)   in relation to her unlawful admission or detention in hospital, the patient's application for a judicial review was granted and appropriate declaratory relief ordered;

(8)   more particularly, however, in relation to the patient's refusal of consent to the medical treatment proposed, the Court of Appeal allowed the patient's appeal against the declaration granted by the judge at first instance. The declaration was set aside ex debito justitiae.

It was held that the judge had erred in making a declaratory order on an ex parte application, in proceedings which had not been instituted by the issue of the summons, without the patient's knowledge or without any attempt to inform her or her solicitor of the application. Further, the order had been made without any evidence and without any provision for the patient to apply to vary or discharge the order.

The consequence generally of an invasion of a person's autonomy without consent may be a cause of action for damages for trespass to the person. For example, in the Canadian case of *Malette v Shulman* [1990] 67 DLR (4d) 321, the court upheld an award of $20,000 to a patient who had been given a blood transfusion in order to save her life but against her known wishes. She was a card-carrying Jehovah's Witness. In the *St George's Healthcare NHS Trust v S* case, the Caesarian section performed on the patient S (together with the accompanying medical procedure) amounted to trespass. Whilst it might be available to defeat any cleam based on aggravated or examplary damages on the particular facts of the case, the Court of Appeal held that the judge's decision at first instance, which was set aside on appeal, would provide no defence to the patient's claim for damages for trespass against the hospital.

Emergency treatment

It is lawful for a doctor to treat an adult of sound mind without his or her consent in an emergency where, for example, as a result of an accident or otherwise, he or she is unconscious and an operation or other treatment cannot be safely delayed until he or she recovers consciousness: *Re F* [1990] 2 AC 1 at 55.

1.3.2 Adults who through lack of capacity are unable to consent to or refuse medical treatment

The basis of any right to treat in the absence of consent
The principles referred to encompass both adults with long-term mental disability and ordinarily competent adults who are found temporarily to be lacking in capacity.

A doctor may treat an adult lacking capacity to consent only in accordance with common law or statute.

The common law principle is that a doctor may lawfully operate on, or give other treatment to, an adult patient who is incapable, for one reason or another, of consenting to the doctor's doing so, provided that the operation or treatment concerned is in the best interests of the patient. The operation or other treatment will be in the patient's best interests if, but only if, it is carried out in order to save his life or to ensure improvement or prevent deterioration in his physical or mental health.

In many cases, it will not only be lawful for doctors to operate on or give other medical treatment to adult patients disabled from giving their consent, it will also be their common law duty to do so: *Re F* [1990] 2 AC 1 at 55, 56.

The common law principle of necessity
The justification in common law for medical intervention and treatment for those patients lacking the capacity to consent, lies in the common law principle of necessity.

In the case of in *Re F* [1990] 2 AC 1, the courts struggled to find the proper basis of jurisdiction for the determination of whether a 36-year-old handicapped woman should have a sterilisation operation. In this regard, the High Court determined that the court was entitled, jurisdictionally, to grant a declaration that such an operation would be lawful as being in her best interests. Lord Goff was of the view that the principle of necessity applied beyond cases of emergency and that the lawfulness of the doctor's action was to be found at least in its origin in the principle of necessity. There was not unanimity in the House of Lords in the case of in *Re F* as to the applicability of the principle of necessity, since the emphasis was on the jurisdiction or question referred to above. Lord Bridge, in *Re F*, was concerned to stress that too rigid a criterion of necessity to determine what is and is not lawful in the treatment of the incompetent would be undesirable since then many of those unfortunate enough to be deprived of the capacity to make rational decisions by accident, illness or unsoundness of mind might be deprived of treatment which it would be entirely beneficial for them to receive.

In *R v Bournewood Community and Mental Health NHS Trust ex parte L* [1998] 2 FLR 550, the adult patient, L, was 48 years old and autistic. He was so profoundly mentally retarded that he was incapable of consenting to medical treatment. The principle question in the case was whether, as a person incapable of consenting to treatment, he could be admitted to hospital for his mental disorder informally under s 131(1) of the Mental Health Act 1983 and thereby without compulsory detention. The House of Lords held that adults who are incapable of consenting may be admitted under s 131(1) for treatment without a compulsory detention.

Since, then, the safeguards provided by the Mental Health Act 1983 to those compulsorily detained would not apply, the question arose as to the justification in law for the medical treatment of those informally admitted to hospital.

It was firmly held that the common law principle of necessity justified the medical treatment of L during his admission and there was fortification for the proposition raised in *Re F* that, generally, the justification in common law for medical intervention and treatment for adults who are unable to consent to such treatment lies in the principle of necessity.

1.3.3 Minors

The parental right to consent to medical treatment for and on behalf of a minor
A doctor is not entitled to treat a patient without the consent of someone who is authorised to give consent.

An immature child is incapable of giving consent to medical treatment, such that a parent or person with parental responsibility will consent on the child's behalf. Until a child achieves the capacity to consent, the right of the parent or the person with parental responsibility to make the decision continues save only in exceptional circumstances. Exceptional circumstances may justify the doctor proceeding to treat the child as a matter of necessity without parental knowledge or consent, such as an emergency, parental neglect, abandonment of the child or the inability to find the parents.

The right of a minor to consent to treatment on his or her own behalf
At common law, a child will be able to consent to medical treatment for and on his own behalf when he achieves a sufficient understanding and intelligence to enable him to understand fully what is proposed. This has become known as meeting the '*Gillick*-competence' test. At the age of 16 years, a minor is provided with a statutory right of consent under s 8 of the Family Law Reform Act 1969.

The concurrent powers of parent and child to consent to treatment
In *Re R (A Minor) (Wardship: Medical Treatment)* [1992] 1 FLR 190 and *Re W (A Minor) (Consent to Medical Treatment)* [1993] 1 FLR 1, the court was concerned with two female minors.

In *Re R* the minor was 15 years old with mental health problems.

In *Re W* the minor had attained the age of 16 years and suffered from anorexia nervosa. Each girl was refusing medical treatment. The issue in each case was the nature and extent of the power of a minor to refuse medical treatment.

The firm view taken by the court was that no minor of whatever age has power, by refusing consent to treatment, to override a consent to treatment on their behalf by a parent or person with parental responsibility for them.

The reasoning is that throughout a child's minority the parental right to consent is retained. It does not determine when the child achieves *Gillick*-competence. Upon the achievement of *Gillick*-competence, the child's power of consent is concurrent with that of the parent or guardian. The consent of either the parent or child may enable treatment to be given lawfully. Only a refusal of consent by all those with the power of consent can create a veto. This means that once a minor is *Gillick*-competent either the minor or parent can give a valid consent to medical treatment of the minor and neither can override the other's consent and exercise a veto.

1.4 NEXT OF KIN

An adult of sound mind will be able to consent to or refuse treatment as he or she wishes. An adult lacking capacity for whatever reason will not be able to do so. No one, including the court, can consent or refuse consent to medical treatment for and on behalf of an adult patient lacking capacity.

Next of kin or relatives may be asked to approve a medical decision made, but the decision itself rests with the doctor acting in the best interests of the patient. It is undoubtedly proper and good practice and humane for the next of kin or close relatives to be consulted and listened to. The legal position, however, is as follows, per Lord Donaldson in *Re T (An Adult) (Consent to Medical Treatment)* [1992] 2 FLR 458 at 461:

> 'There seems to be a view in the medical profession that in such emergency circumstances the next of kin should be asked to consent on behalf of the patient and that, if possible, treatment should be postponed until that consent has been obtained. This is a misconception because the next of kin has no legal right either to consent or to refuse consent.'

What may emanate, however, from consultation with the next of kin or close relatives is whether the patient has made an advance statement or 'living will' orally or in writing expressing his specific wishes, if any, in relation to medical treatment including, for example, refusal of any form of medical treatment or otherwise. As to living wills, see Chapter 9.

Chapter 2

THE 'BEST INTERESTS OF THE PATIENT' TEST

2.1   ADULTS OF SOUND MIND

Pursuant to the principle of self-determination, if an adult of sound mind refuses, however unreasonably, to consent to treatment or care, the doctors responsible for his care must give effect to his wishes, even though they do not consider it to be in his best interests to do so: *Airedale NHS Trust v Bland* [1993] AC 789, HL at 864.

2.2   ADULTS WHO ARE UNABLE TO CONSENT TO OR REFUSE MEDICAL TREATMENT

A doctor can lawfully operate on or give other treatment to adult patients who are incapable, for one reason or another, of consenting to his doing so, provided that the operation or other treatment concerned is in the best interests of the patient. The operation or other treatment will be in the patient's best interests if, but only if, it is carried out in order either to save their lives or to ensure improvement or prevent deterioration in their physical or mental health: *Re F* [1990] 2 AC 1 at 55.

The standard of care of any such medical treatment is be judged by the test laid down in *Bolam v Friern Hospital Management Committee* [1957] 1 WLR 582, per Lord Goff in *Re F (Mental Patient: Sterilisation)* [1990] 2 AC 1 at 78:

> 'I have said that the doctor has to act in the best interests of the assisted person. In the case of routine treatment of mentally disordered persons, there should be little difficulty in applying this principle. In the case of more serious treatment, I recognise that its application may create problems for the medical profession; however, in making decisions about treatment, the doctor must act in accordance with a responsible and competent body of relevant professional opinion on the principles set out in *Bolam* ...'

2.3   MINORS

There is only one test. The court's prime and paramount consideration is the best interests of the minor: *Re J (A Minor) (Wardship: Medical Treatment)* [1991] 1 FLR 366.

The court performs a balancing act bringing all the relevant expert evidence and other evidence before it so as to enable the court to decide whether the proposed treatment is or is not in the minor's best interests.

The parents' view must be weighed and heeded, yet they cannot prevail over the court's view of the ward's best interests.

The decisions by the court as to medical treatment will often be made within the inherent jurisdiction of the High Court in its parens patriae function.

There are circumstances, however, where the Children Act 1989 will be appropriate for a decision. A parent may seek, for example, a specific issue order under s 8 of the Act. In care proceedings, a decision may have to be made under s 38(6) as to medical examinations or other assessments of the child. In these circumstances, the terms of the Act must apply. These include the paramountcy test and checklist factors under s 1 of the Act.

2.4   THE PRINCIPLE OF THE SANCTITY OF LIFE

The principle of the sanctity of life is a fundamental principle and recognised internationally both in Article 2 of the European Convention for the Protection of Human Rights and Fundamental Freedoms (1953) (Cmd 8969), and in Article 6 of the International Covenant of Civil and Political Rights 1966.

In any case involving medical treatment, the court's high respect for the sanctity of human life imposes a strong presumption in favour of taking all steps capable of preserving it.

The principle, however, is not an absolute one. It does not compel a medical practitioner to treat a patient, who will die if he does not give treatment, contrary to the expressed wishes of the patient. It does not authorise forcible feeding of prisoners who are competent and on hunger strike. It does not compel the temporary keeping alive of patients who are terminally ill where to do so would merely prolong their suffering. On the other hand, it forbids the taking of active measures to cut short the life of a terminally ill patient: *Airedale NHS Trust v Bland* [1993] AC 789, HL at 859.

2.5   PROLONGATION OF LIFE MAY NOT BE IN THE BEST INTERESTS OF THE PATIENT

It is emphasised in various decisions that the preservation and sanctity of life is presumed to be of the highest importance by the courts. Notwithstanding this presumption, prolongation of life cannot be and is not the sole objective of the courts:

'The doctor who is caring for ... a patient cannot, in my opinion, be under an absolute obligation to prolong his life by any means available to him, regardless of the quality of the patient's life. Common humanity requires otherwise, as do medical ethics and good medical practice ...' *Airedale NHS Trust v Bland* [1993] AC 789 at 867.

In *Re J (A Minor) (Wardship: Medical Treatment)* [1991] 1 FLR 366, the Court of Appeal considered the case of a child born prematurely with serious brain damage and who originally required resuscitation by means of mechanical ventilation. The child thereafter suffered convulsions, episodes when he stopped breathing and again was placed on a ventilator. The court at first instance approved the recommendation of the consultant neurologist in charge of the case that, in the event of further convulsions requiring resuscitation, the child should not be revived by means of mechanical ventilation unless to do so seemed appropriate to those involved in his care in that situation. The Court of Appeal dismissed an appeal against that decision. It was held that, although there was a strong presumption in favour of the preservation of life, no principle of public policy regarding the sanctity of life displaced the paramountcy of the best interests of the child in question. Lord Taylor LJ said at p 381B:

'The plight of baby J is appalling and the problem facing the court in the exercise of its wardship jurisdiction is of the greatest difficulty. When should the court rule against the giving of treatment aimed at prolonging life?'.

At p 383H, he further said:

'I consider the correct approach is for the court to judge the quality of life the child would have to endure if given the treatment, and decide whether in all the circumstances such a life would be so afflicted as to be intolerable to that child'.

The approach of Lord Taylor was echoed by Sir Stephen Brown, the President of the Family Division, in *Re R* [1996] 2 FLR 99 at 107. The test throughout adopted by the court is to determine what is in the best interests of the patient. In *Re R*, the court made clear that the test was the same whether the patient was a child or, as in that case, an adult who was critically handicapped.

The extent of the dilemma for the courts as to what may be in the best interests of a patient is evidenced by the case of *Re T (Wardship: Medical Treatment)* [1997] 1 FLR 502. The Court of Appeal there emphasised that to prolong life was not the sole objective of the court and to require it at the expense of other considerations might not be in a child's best interests. Butler-Sloss LJ took the view that the mother and baby 'were one for the purpose of this unusual case'. The baby was suffering from a life-threatening liver defect and, without a transplant, would not live beyond the age of two and a half. The medical opinion was that the prospects of success of a transplant were good. The parents did not wish the operation to take place. The issue for the court was whether to give consent for the operation and thereby to overrule the decision of the parents. The mother, knowing that the baby had only a short time to live if no operation was performed, had focused on the present peaceful life of the baby without the pain, stress and upset of intrusive surgery against a future with the operation and treatment taking place. The conclusion of the Court of Appeal was that the baby's best interests required that his future treatment be left in the hands of his parents.

2.6   THE WITHDRAWAL OF LIFE-SUSTAINING TREATMENT AND THE BEST INTERESTS OF THE PATIENT

Any decision whether or not to withhold or withdraw life-sustaining treatment in the absence of clear instructions from the patient himself or herself, must be made in the best interests of the patient.

There are two categories in which to consider the patient's best interests.

There are cases in which, having regard to all the circumstances, including in particular the poor quality of life which may be prolonged for the patient if the treatment is successful, it may be judged not to be in the patient's best interests to provide it or to continue to provide it. *Re J (A Minor) (Wardship: Medical Treatment)* [1991] 1 FLR 366, is an example of this type of case. It concerned a child who suffered severe brain damage. The most optimistic view was that he would develop spastic quadriplegia, that he was likely to be blind and deaf, that he would never be able to speak or develop even limited intellectual abilities. He was not dying or on the point of death. He had previously spent periods on a ventilator. The question was what should be done if baby J suffered another collapse. The doctors unanimously recommended that, in that event, there should be no mechanical re-ventilation on the basis that it was an invasive and painful procedure which might itself cause deterioration and at best could only bring about minimal improvement. The Court of Appeal endorsed the decision at first instance, holding that it would not be in the child's best interests to subject him to a mechanical ventilator if he stopped breathing, whilst at the same time leaving the doctors free to take more active measures to preserve the child's life if the situation improved. In this category of case, the court will weigh up all the relevant considerations and reach a decision as to whether the proposed medical treatment is in the best interests of the patient.

In *Re J*, Taylor LJ at p 383H summarised his approach to the weighing exercise:

> 'I consider the correct approach is for the Court to judge the quality of life the child would have to endure if given the treatment, and decide whether in all the circumstances such a life would be so afflicted as to be intolerable to that child. I say "to that child" because the test should not be whether the life would be tolerable to the decider. The test must be whether the child in question, if capable of exercising sound judgment, would consider the life tolerable. This is the approach adopted by McKenzie J in *Re Superintendent of Family and Child Service and Dawson* [1983] 145 DLR (3d) 610 in the passage at page 620 …'

There are cases such as that of Anthony Bland where life-sustaining treatment can be of no benefit to the patient because he is totally insensate and there is no prospect of improvement in his condition. As was said in the House of Lords in *Airedale NHS Trust v Bland* [1993] AC 789, in this situation there is in reality no weighing operation to be performed. The justification and lawfulness for the initial life-sustaining treatment in *Bland* was the hope and expectation that there might be some improvement in the patient's condition or hope of recovery, however imperfect. Pursuant to the rationale and reasoning in *Re F (Mental Patient: Sterilisation)* [1990] 2 AC 1, it was lawful and it was the duty of the doctors to treat Anthony Bland accordingly in his best interests by taking all steps to preserve his life. However, once the justification for such medical treatment was gone, because there was no prospect of recovery or improvement, it could no longer be the duty of the doctors, nor perhaps was it lawful for them, to continue such medical treatment as being in his best interest:

> 'If I am right so far in my analysis, the critical decision to be made is whether it is in the best interests of Anthony Bland to continue the invasive medical care involved in artificial feeding. That question is not the same as, 'is it in Anthony Bland's best interests that he should die?' The latter question assumes that it is lawful to perpetuate the patient's life: such perpetuation of life can only be achieved if it is lawful to continue to invade the bodily integrity of the patient by invasive medical care. Unless the doctor has reached the affirmative conclusion that it is in the patient's best interests to continue the invasive care, such care must cease': per Lord Browne-Wilkinson, *Airedale NHS Trust v Bland* [1993] AC 789, HL at 884.

2.7 THE LAW COMMISSION'S SUGGESTED TEST OF 'BEST INTERESTS'

Within the Law Commission Report 231 on mental incapacity is a Draft of a Bill to make new provision in relation to mentally incapacitated persons. The relevant provisions are reproduced in Part III of this book. Although this Draft Bill is not as yet on the statute book, it is helpful to scrutinise cl 3 of the Draft Bill which sets out a proposed 'best interests of the patient' test:

> '3(1) anything done for, and any decision made on behalf of, a person by virtue of this Part of this Act shall be done or made in his best interests.
> (2) in deciding what is in a person's best interests regard shall be had to the following—
> (a) so far as ascertainable, his past and present wishes and feelings and the factors which he would consider if he were able to do so;
> (b) the need to permit and encourage that person to participate, or to improve his ability to participate, as fully as possible in anything done for and any decision affecting him;
> (c) if it is practicable and appropriate to consult them, the views as to that person's wishes and feelings and as to what would be in his best interests of—
> (i) any person named by him as someone to be consulted on those matters;
> (ii) anyone [whether his spouse, a relative, friend or other person] engaged in caring for him or interested in his welfare;

(iii) the donee of any continuing power of attorney granted by him;

(iv) any manager appointed for him by the court;

(d) whether the purpose for which any action or decision is required can be as effectively achieved in a manner less restrictive of his freedom of action ...'

Chapter 3

THE DOCTOR AND THE COURTS

3.1 THE INTERFACE BETWEEN THE DOCTOR AND THE COURTS

The relationship between and the respective roles of the doctor and the courts is well and succinctly set out by Lord Goff in *Airedale NHS Trust v Bland* [1993] AC 789, HL at 871 as follows:

> 'The truth is that, in the course of their work, doctors frequently have to make decisions which may affect the continued survival of their patients, and are in reality far more experienced in matters of this kind than are the judges. It is nevertheless the function of the judges to state the legal principles upon which the lawfulness of the actions of doctors depend; but in the end the decisions to be made in individual cases must rest with the doctors themselves. In these circumstances, what is required is a sensitive understanding by both the judges and the doctors of each other's respective functions, and in particular a determination by the judges not merely to understand the problems facing the medical profession in cases of this kind, but also to regard their professional standards with respect. Mutual understanding between the doctors and the judges is the best way to ensure the evolution of a sensitive and sensible legal framework for the treatment and care of patients, with a sound ethical base, in the interest of the patients themselves.'

3.2 THE OBJECTIVES OF MEDICAL TREATMENT AND CARE

The objectives of medical treatment and care are to benefit the patient. They include:

(i) preventing the occurrence of injury, deformity or other illness before they occur;
(ii) to cure illness when it does occur;
(iii) where illness cannot be cured, to prevent or retard deterioration of the patient's condition;
(iv) to relieve pain and suffering in body and mind.

Since the advance of medical technology, the question has arisen as to whether and to what extent it is or should be an object of medical treatment to prolong a patient's life by any means available to the doctor, regardless of the quality of the patient's life.

The meaning of medical treatment for the purposes of the Act is set out in s 145 of the Mental Health Act 1983.

The statutory duty of the Secretary of State to provide treatment and facilities for the prevention of illness and the cure of persons suffering from that illness are set out under s 1(1) and s 3(1) of the National Health Service Act 1977. Section 13 of the Act provides for directions to be given to health authorities to exercise on the Secretary of State's behalf such functions under the statute relating to the Health Service as he may specify.

3.3   THE DUTY OF THE DOCTOR

A medical practitioner owes a fundamental duty to his or her patient, subject to obtaining any necessary consent, to treat the patient in accordance with his or her own best clinical judgment: in *Re J (A Minor) (Medical Treatment)* [1992] 2 FLR 165 at 172, 173.

However, such a duty to act in his or her patient's best interests will be qualified if an adult patient of sound mind refuses, however unreasonably, to consent to treatment or care. Even if the effect of the refusal may be serious damage to the patient's health or, at worst, death, the doctor responsible for his or her care must give effect to his or her wishes, even though he or she does not consider it to be in the patient's best interests to do so. It has been held, for example, in *Nancy B v Hotel-Dieu De Quebec* [1992] 86 DLR (4d) 385, that a patient of sound mind may, if properly informed, require that life support should be discontinued. The basis in law for qualifying the doctor's duty accordingly is that the principle of the sanctity of human life must yield to the principle of self-determination.

The doctor's duty must also be qualified where the patient's refusal to give his consent to treatment has been expressed at an earlier date (before, for example, he became unconscious or otherwise incapable of communicating it); although, in such circumstances, special care may be necessary to ensure that the prior refusal of consent is still properly to be regarded as applicable in the circumstances which have subsequently occurred: *Airedale NHS Trust v Bland* [1993] AC 789, HL at 864.

It is recognised in relation to the duty of a doctor that the function of a doctor per Lord Donaldson in *Re J (A Minor) (Medical Treatment)* [1992] 2 FLR 165 at 173:

> 'is not a limited technical one of repairing or servicing a body. They are treating people in a real life context'.

3.3.1   The standard of care by a doctor in relation to medical treatment

The standard of care required of a doctor and, subject to obtaining any necessary consent, is that laid down in *Bolam v Friern Hospital Management Committee*

[1957] 1 WLR 582, namely that a patient should be treated or cared for in accordance with good medical practice recognised as appropriate by a competent body of professional opinion.

3.3.2   No doctor can be required to treat a patient (whether adult or minor) in a particular way and against his or her clinical judgment

In *Re C (Medical Treatment)* [1998] 1 FLR 384, Sir Stephen Brown, President of the Family Division, was concerned with a girl aged 16 months who was suffering from a desperately serious disease. It was a 'no chance' situation within the *Framework of Practice: Withholding or Withdrawing Life-Saving Treatment in Children* published by the Royal College of Paediatrics and Child Health.

Her disease was so severe that life-sustaining treatment would simply delay death without significantly alleviating suffering. The doctors, accordingly, wished to withdraw ventilation and did not believe that reinstating ventilation, even in the highly probable event of the child's further respiratory relapse, would be in her best interests. The parents were prepared for ventilation to be withdrawn to see whether C would survive without it, but wished it to be reinstated in the event of further respiratory relapse. The hospital sought and was granted the court's approval for the withdrawal of ventilation and non-resuscitation in the event of respiratory arrest. The President of the Family Division was unwilling to require the doctors to undertake a course of treatment which they themselves were unwilling to undertake.

In *Re R (A Minor)* [1992] 1 FLR 190, CA at 200, Lord Donaldson said:

> 'No doctor can be required to treat a child, whether by the court in the exercise of its wardship jurisdiction, by the parents, by the child or anyone else. The decision whether to treat is dependent upon an exercise of his own professional judgment, subject only to the threshold requirement that, save in exceptional cases usually of emergency, he has the consent of someone who has authority to give that consent.'

In *Re J (A Minor) (Wardship: Medical Treatment)* [1991] 1 FLR 366 at 370, again Lord Donaldson put the matter as follows:

> 'No one can *dictate* the treatment to be given to the child – neither court, parents nor doctors. There are checks and balances. The doctors can recommend treatment A in preference to treatment B. They can also refuse to adopt treatment C on the grounds that it is medically contraindicated, or for some other reason is a treatment which they could not conscientiously administer. The court or parents, for their part, can refuse to consent to treatment A or B or both, but cannot insist upon treatment C. The inevitable and desirable result is that choice of treatment is, in some measure, a joint decision of the doctors and the court or parents.'

In *Re J (A Minor) (Medical Treatment)* [1992] 2 FLR 165, the court was concerned with a child aged 16 months who was severely handicapped both mentally and physically. His expectation of life was short. He was with foster parents. His breathing was assisted by oxygen. The consultant paediatrician in charge of his case said that it was not medically appropriate to intervene with intensive therapeutic measures such as artificial ventilation if the child were to suffer a life-threatening event. The local authority, supported by the mother, asked the court to require the health authority to continue to provide all available treatment, including 'intensive resuscitation'. The local authority was granted an interim injunction by a judge requiring the health authority, if the baby suffered a life-threatening collapse, to 'cause such measures (including, if so required to prolong his life, artificial ventilation) to be applied to the child for so long as they are capable of prolonging his life'.

This order was set aside by the Court of Appeal and Lord Justice Balcombe said at p 175:

> '... I agree with the Master of the Rolls that I can conceive of no situation where it would be a proper exercise of the jurisdiction to make such an order as was made in the present case: that is to order a doctor, whether directly or indirectly, to treat a child in a manner contrary to his or her clinical judgment. I would go further. I find it difficult to conceive of a situation where it would be a proper exercise of the jurisdiction to make an order positively requiring a doctor to adopt a particular course of treatment in relation to a child, unless the doctor himself or herself was asking the Court to make such an order. Usually all the Court is asked, or needs to do is to authorise a particular course of treatment where the person or body whose consent is requisite is unable or unwilling to do so.'

3.4   ALLOCATION OF RESOURCES AND THE CHOICE OF MEDICATION

This aspect in relation to medical treatment was raised in the case of *R v Cambridge District Health Authority ex parte B* [1995] 1 FLR 1055. The facts were as follows. In January of 1995, the child, aged 10 years, suffered a relapse of acute myeloid leukaemia. Since first becoming ill, five years previously, she had been treated with two courses of chemotherapy, total body irradiation and a bone marrow transplant. The doctors who had treated her and other experts consulted by them were of the opinion that the child had a very short time to live and that no further treatment could usefully be administered. Unwilling to accept that view, the father obtained further medical opinion to the effect that a further course of chemotherapy might be undertaken with a chance of success estimated at 10 per cent to 20 per cent at a cost of £15,000, followed, if that was successful, by a second transplant with a similar chance of success, at a cost of £60,000. The respondent district health authority, taking into account that assessment together with the opinion of the child's medical advisers and the Department of Health guidelines on the funding of treatment not of a proven nature, stated that it was unwilling to fund further treatment. Its decision was based on two grounds. First, that the proposed treatment would cause considerable suffering and not be in the child's best interests. Secondly, that the substantial expenditure on treatment with such a small prospect of success and of an experimental nature would not be an effective use of limited resources, bearing in mind the present and future needs of other patients. The child applied by her father as next friend by way of judicial review for an order of certiorari quashing that decision. The judge at first instance allowed the application and quashed the respondent's decision. The district health authority appealed. The Court of Appeal reversed the judge's decision and allowed the appeal of the district health authority.

The Court of Appeal made quite clear that, in judicial review proceedings, the only function of the court was to rule upon the lawfulness of the decision. The courts could not be arbiters as to the merits of cases of this kind. The powers of the court, it was held, were not such as to enable it to substitute its own decision in a matter of this kind for that of the health authority which was legally charged with making the decision. The Court of Appeal was unable to say that the district health authority, on the particular facts, had acted in a way that exceeded its powers or which was unreasonable in the legal sense.

It is clear, and important to note, that funding was not raised as the issue in itself which lay behind the district health authority's decision. Insofar as it was raised as a factor, and no doubt an important factor, the authority took into account the Department of Health guidelines on the funding of treatment not of a proven nature. The treatment of the child proposed by the father was described by Sir Thomas Bingham MR in the Court of Appeal as being 'at the frontier of medical science', even if the word 'experimental' was not the appropriate word: it was a treatment, he said, unlike many courses of treatment, which did not have a well-tried track record of success.

The decision of the district health authority was based on an amalgam of factors, a clinical assessment by the child's medical advisers and an assessment of the medical treatment proposed by the father, the child's welfare as well as the funding element.

Sir Thomas Bingham MR, in the Court of Appeal, was certainly willing to entertain the consideration that difficulties in financial resources could legitimately be raised as a factor in the decision by the health authority:

'I have no doubt that in a perfect world any treatment which a patient, or a patient's family, sought would be provided if doctors were willing to give it, no matter how much it cost, particularly when a life was potentially at stake. It would however, in my view, be shutting one's eyes to the real world if the court were to proceed on the basis that we do live in such a world. It is common knowledge that health authorities of all kinds are constantly pressed to make ends meet. They cannot pay their nurses as much as they would like; they cannot provide all the treatments they would like; they cannot purchase all the extremely expensive medical equipment they would like; they cannot carry out all the research they would like; they cannot build all the hospitals and specialist units they would like. Difficult and agonising judgments have to be made as to how a limited budget is best allocated to the maximum advantage of the maximum number of patients. That is not a judgment which the court can make. In my judgment, it is not something that a health authority such as this authority can be fairly criticised for not advancing before the court.'

It is trite but nevertheless an important point to make that, insofar as the allocation of resources is raised in any case before the courts, the weight to be given to such issue, accordingly, will depend on the particular facts of the case and the reasons for any decisions made.

References in case-law are scant to the question of the allocation of resources and conflicting choices. It is to be noted that, obiter in *Re J (A Minor) (Wardship: Medical Treatment)* [1991] 1 FLR 366, CA at 370G, Lord Donaldson said:

'In an imperfect world, resources will always be limited and on occasion agonising choices will have to be made in allocating those resources to particular patients'.

The question of the allocation of limited healthcare resources was, however, central to the case of *R v North West Lancashire Health Authority ex parte A, D and G*, as yet unreported, and in which judgment was given in the High Court on 21 December 1998. The applicants were three transsexuals who were challenging the decision of the health authority in question not to fund gender re-assignment treatment for themselves, including surgery for the removal of the male sex organs. The court was requested to consider policy documents of the authority, including one which listed a number of procedures which would not be purchased 'except in cases of overriding clinical need'. These included gender re-assignment, cosmetic plastic surgery and reversal of sterilisation. The applicants' case was that they had, on medical advice, a demonstrable clinical need for the required surgery and treatment and that the health authority's policy (despite the wording 'except in cases of overriding clinical need') was in reality a blanket ban on such treatment. The health authority's case, again on medical advice, was that there was no 'overriding clinical need' which would justify the allocation of its limited resources to the treatment requested. The judge accepted that, on the authorities, it was not for the court to seek to allocate scarce resources in a tight budget. The court was, however, entitled to consider the lawfulness of the authority's decision and policy in the context of the authority's duty to exercise on behalf of the Secretary of State duties under s 1(1) and 3(1) of the National Health Service Act 1977. These include the duty to provide treatment and facilities for the prevention of illness and the cure of persons suffering from such illness. Much evidence turned on the nature, medically, of transsexualism or Gender Identity Dysphoria (GID) and the proper treatment for it. The judge concluded that the health authority had reached its decisions without sufficient consideration of the question of what is proper treatment for what is recognised as an illness. Further, the court determined that the decisions and policy, including the words 'except in cases of overriding clinical need' – unclear and uncertain as they were – unlawfully fettered the authority's exercise of its discretion in discharging its statutory duty referred to above to provide medical treatment. Accordingly, the authority was held to have acted unlawfully and irrationally in its decisions and relief was granted in judicial review as sought by the applicants. The application of the authority for leave to appeal to the Court of Appeal was refused by the judge, on the basis that, if any such leave was to be sought, application would have accordingly to be made to the Court of Appeal.

Chapter 4

THE JURISDICTION OF THE COURTS TO INTERVENE IN RELATION TO THE MEDICAL TREATMENT OF ADULTS AND MINORS

4.1 DECLARATORY RELIEF UNDER THE INHERENT JURISDICTION OF THE HIGH COURT IN RELATION TO INCAPACITATED ADULTS

4.1.1 *Re F* and the court's jurisdiction in relation to incapacitated adults

In *Re F (Sterilisation: Mental Patient)* [1990] 2 AC 1 concerned a 36-year-old mentally handicapped woman, F, who resided in a mental hospital as a voluntary in-patient. Her mother issued an originating summons for a declaration that a sterilisation operation would not amount to an unlawful act by reason only of the absence of F's consent.

The Court of Appeal took the view that, through an amended RSC, Ord 80, the court was able to 'approve' or 'disapprove' the proposed medical treatment, namely the sterilisation operation.

In the House of Lords, there was painstaking and detailed consideration of the jurisdiction that might be available to permit the court to decide the case. The difficulties jurisdictionally were these:

(i)   there was no statutory basis for authorising the sterilisation;
(ii) the court was not able to assume any rights and duties in relation to the patient since the parens patriae jurisdiction was no longer exercisable by the courts in relation to adults of unsound mind. At p 55 of *Re F*, Lord Brandon indicated how straightforward, jurisdictionally, the situation would have been had F been 17 and not 36 years of age, since then an originating summons would have been issued in wardship and the court would then have been exercising its parens patriae jurisdiction;
(iii) there was no common law rule permitting 'approval' or, 'disapproval' of the proposed operation.

The solution of the House of Lords in *Re F* was that there was jurisdiction for the court, as part of its inherent jurisdiction, to grant a declaration as to the lawfulness of the proposed medical treatment. Any declaration issued should be sought under RSC, Ord 15, r 16, yet that provision in the Rules does not in itself confer upon the court any jurisdiction. What confers jurisdiction to grant declaratory relief is the inherent jurisdiction of the High Court.

The implications following *Re F* of the nature of such jurisdiction in relation to incapacitated adults are as follows:

(i)   whilst the 'best interests of patient test' will be at the forefront of the court's mind in such a case (as would be so in relation to the case of a minor), the court is not able to approve or disapprove of medical treatment in relation to an incapacitated adult;

(ii) no one, including the court, can consent or refuse to consent to medical treatment on behalf of an adult who lacks capacity;

(iii) it follows that the next of kin have no legal right to consent or refuse consent on behalf of the patient in relation to medical treatment;

(iv) decisions as to medical treatment rest with medical practitioners who, in the absence of consent, may treat the adult patient who is incapacitated, provided such treatment is in the patient's best interests;

(v)   the court has jurisdiction to declare whether proposed medical treatment for an adult patient lacking capacity is lawful as being in the patient's best interests;

(vi) any originating summons so issued must be appropriately worded to seek from the court a declaration that the medical treatment proposed, in the absence of the patient's consent, is not unlawful as being in his best interests.

4.1.2   The broad approach to declaratory relief in the Family Division

The case of *Re S (Hospital Patient: Court's Jurisdiction)* [1995] 1 FLR 1075 is important in this regard. The patient, a Norwegian national, married his Norwegian wife in 1945. Their son was born in 1947. In 1989, the patient met another lady, the plaintiff. She accompanied him on his travels and he gave her power of attorney entitling her to operate some of his bank accounts. In 1991, they set up house together in England. In 1993, the patient suffered a severe stroke which left him with right-sided hemiplegia and severely impaired communication skills. The plaintiff secured his admission to hospital, paying his account under her power of attorney. She visited him regularly and showed close interest in his welfare. The wife and son visited, although less frequently, and in 1994 the son attempted to remove the patient from the hospital to the airport for a flight to Norway, without giving notice to the hospital authorities or to the plaintiff. The plaintiff alerted the police and obtained an interlocutory injunction, and as a result the patient was returned to the hospital. The proceedings in which the plaintiff claimed declaratory relief were transferred to the Family Division. The plaintiff filed evidence that the patient wished to remain in England close to her, eventually in their own home, while the wife and son, the second and first defendants, contended that he would be happier with them. The procedural question as to whether the court had jurisdiction to grant declaratory relief to the plaintiff was argued before the judge in the Family Division who held that, as regards the locus of the plaintiff, if it had been necessary to show that her own legal position would be resolved by the granting of the declaration, that requirement was satisfied. Had it not been necessary for the proposed relief to concern the plaintiff's own legal position, her relationship with the patient, her access to his funds and her desire to care for him amounted to sufficient interest on her part for her to seek declaratory relief. Accordingly, the judge found for the plaintiff, but, since it was the court's aim to preserve the status quo while proper enquiries were made, granted an interim injunction to prevent the patient's removal from hospital until trial or further order. The first and second defendants appealed, contending that the court had no jurisdiction to grant relief to the plaintiff in cases where there was no legal relationship between the parties.

The Court of Appeal, in dismissing the appeal, held that, where there was controversy as to the care of the patient who, as in the present case, was rendered unconscious or inarticulate by sudden illness and who could not express his preference, the court treated as justiciable any question as to the patient's best interests. Moreover, where a serious justiciable issue was brought before the court by a party with a genuine and legitimate interest in obtaining a decision against an adverse party, the court would not impose neat tests to determine the precise legal standing of the claimant. Had it been necessary for the plaintiff to demonstrate, in herself, a specifically legal right which was liable to be infringed by the proposed action of the wife and son, the plaintiff in the circumstances of the case had done so, but, in any event, the matters listed by the judge which showed that the plaintiff was far from being a stranger or an officious busybody were enough to give the court jurisdiction.

The broad approach in the Family Division that the court's jurisdiction to grant declaratory relief should not easily be defeated on purely procedural grounds is exemplified in the judgment of Sir Thomas Bingham at p 1087G–H of *Re S*:

> 'In none of the cases cited to us has an applicant for declaratory relief failed on purely procedural grounds. Thus the Royal College of Nursing, Mrs Gillick, doctors, hospital authorities and relatives (whether next friend of the patient or not) have all obtained relief or been held entitled in principle to do so. It cannot of course be suggested that any stranger or officious busybody, however remotely connected with the patient or with the subject matter of proceedings, can properly seek or obtain declaratory or any other relief (in private law any more than public law proceedings). But it can be suggested that where a serious justiciable issue is brought before the court by a party with a genuine and legitimate interest in obtaining a decision against an adverse party the court will not impose nice tests to determine the precise legal standing of that claimant.'

4.1.3 The Court of Protection

The Court of Protection is concerned with the management of the property and affairs of patients under the Mental Health Act 1983. The House of Lords in *Re F* took the view that Part VII of the 1983 Act did not confer on a judge nominated under s 93(1) of the Act any jurisdiction to decide questions relating to the medical treatment of a patient.

4.2 THE COURT'S JURISDICTION IN RELATION TO MINORS

4.2.1 The Children Act 1989

Applications may be made under the Children Act 1989 in relation to the medical treatment of minors. One example may be an application for a specific issue order under s 8 of the 1989 Act where there is a dispute between parents over proposed medical treatment. Another example is care proceedings initiated by a local authority where the court is invited to give directions as to a medical or psychiatric assessment of the child pursuant to s 38(6) of the 1989 Act.

Such applications are governed by Part IV of the Family Proceedings Rules 1991 (FPR 1991).

4.2.2 Parens patriae and the inherent jurisdiction of the High Court in relation to minors

This jurisdiction is examined in more detail in Chapter 8 of this book. The approach, jurisdictionally, is different from that of incapacitated adults. The court, through its parens patriae jurisdiction, is able to step into the shoes of the parents and approve or not approve, for and on behalf of the child, the medical treatment proposed for him or her. The powers of the High Court in relation to minors under its inherent jurisdiction are said to be 'theoretically limitless'. It is a procedure which involves the collation of all the evidence and the court determining what is in the best interests of the minor.

Proceedings under the inherent jurisdiction are assigned to the Family Division and governed generally by the Rules of the Supreme Court 1965 (RSC) and the FPR 1991. Part V of the FPR 1991 sets out the procedure to be followed when applying for wardship. An application to make a minor a ward of court is made by originating summons, together with an affidavit in support. The parens patriae jurisdiction is equally exercisable whether the child is or is not a ward of court. There is no specific provision made in the Rules for cases to be brought under the inherent jurisdiction of the High Court other than in wardship. The appropriate method of commencing proceedings under the inherent jurisdiction other than in wardship is by way of Originating Summons entitled 'In the Matter of the Inherent Jurisdiction'. To all intents and purposes, however, normally applications to the court under the inherent jurisdiction in relation to minors should be made within wardship proceedings.

4.2.3   Local authorities and applications under the inherent jurisdiction

Under s 100(3) of the Children Act 1989, no application for any exercise of the court's inherent jurisdiction with respect to children may be made by a local authority unless the authority has obtained the leave of the court.

It is helpful to set out the statutory provision as to the circumstances in which leave may be given to a local authority to apply for the exercise of the court's inherent jurisdiction.

Under s 100(4), the court may grant leave only if it is satisfied that:

'(a) the result which the authority wish to achieve could not be achieved through the making of any order of a kind to which subsection (5) applies; and
(b) There is reasonable cause to believe that if the court's inherent jurisdiction is not exercised with respect to the child he is likely to suffer significant harm.'

Section 100(5) applies to any order:

'(a) made otherwise than in the exercise of the court's inherent jurisdiction; and
(b) which the local authority is entitled to apply for (assuming, in the case of any application which may only be made with leave, that leave is granted).'

4.3   NEXT FRIEND: GUARDIAN AD LITEM

4.3.1   Specified proceedings under the Children Act 1989

In relation to 'specified' proceedings as defined in s 41(6) of the Children Act 1989, the appointment of a guardian ad litem for the child is governed by r 4.10 of the FPR 1991.

4.3.2   Proceedings in relation to incapacitated adults and in relation to minors other than specified proceedings within the meaning of s 41(6) of the Children Act 1989

Whilst the wider applicable provision is RSC Ord 80, in family proceedings the most relevant rule is r 9 of the FPR 1991.

Under r 9.1 of the FPR 1991, 'patient' means a person who, by reason of mental disorder within the meaning of the Mental Health Act 1983, is incapable of managing and administering his property and affairs.

Further, under r 9.1 of the FPR 1991, a 'person under disability' means a person who is a minor or a patient as defined above.

Under r 9.2(1) of the FPR 1991:

'Except where Rule 9.2A or any other rule otherwise provides, a person under disability may begin and prosecute any Family Proceedings only by his next friend and may defend any such proceedings only by his guardian ad litem and, except as otherwise provided by this Rule, it shall not be necessary for a guardian ad litem to be appointed by the Court.'

Rule 9.2A of the FPR 1991 contains provision for minors, in certain circumstances, to begin to prosecute or defend any proceedings without a next friend or guardian ad litem. Such provision is examined more closely in Chapter 8 of this book.

4.3.3   The Official Solicitor

The Official Solicitor is now an officer of the Supreme Court appointed by the Lord Chancellor under s 90 of the Supreme Court Act 1981.

The Official Solicitor has a number of roles, including the representation of children and incapacitated adults in family proceedings, as follows. He may be invited by the court to act pursuant to r 9.2 of the FPR 1991 as next friend or guardian ad litem on behalf of a 'person under a disability' in family proceedings concerning such a person (whether a minor or patient as defined in r 9.1 of the FPR 1991).

In relation to adults, a patient may be incapable of giving instructions to his solicitors or incapable of managing his property and affairs.

It is a matter for the Official Solicitor in relation to adults and minors whether he accepts or declines any such invitation to so act as a next friend or guardian ad litem.

The Practice Note governing the appointment of the Official Solicitor in family proceedings of December 1998 [1999] 1 FLR 310 is reproduced in Part III of this book. In relation to family proceedings concerning medical treatment, the Official Solicitor will normally be invited to act as guardian ad litem for the patient in declarations seeking leave to withhold or withdraw life-sustaining treatment, where obviously the patient will not be able to speak or act for himself or herself. Set out in Part III of this book is *Practice Note: Official Solicitor to the Supreme Court: 'Vegetative State'* [1996] 2 FLR 375. This Note indicates the central and important role taken by the Official Solicitor in these type of proceedings. Paragraph 8 of the Note adds that, in any case in which the Official Solicitor does not represent the patient, he should be joined as a defendant or respondent.

The Official Solicitor will normally be invited to act as guardian ad litem for the patient in any declaration sought to authorise the sterilisation of a woman who lacks capacity. There are then circumstances where an issue may arise, often urgently, about a patient's competence to consent to or refuse medical treatment. Chapter 6 of this book considers the capacity or lack of capacity of an adult patient to consent to or refuse medical treatment. In *St George's Healthcare NHS Trust v S; R v Collins and Others ex parte S* [1998] 2 FLR 728 at 758, the Court of Appeal has set out detailed guidelines applicable to any case involving capacity when surgical or invasive treatment may be needed by a patient, whether female or male, where there is a real concern about his or her competence to consent to or refuse treatment. These guidelines are reproduced in Part III of this book. At (vi) of these guidelines, it was stated that, if the patient in question is unwilling to instruct solicitors, or is believed to be incapable of doing so, the health authority or its legal advisers must notify the Official Solicitor and invite him to act as guardian ad litem. If the Official Solicitor agrees, he will wish, if possible, to arrange for the patient to be interviewed to ascertain her wishes and to explore the reasons for any refusal of treatment. Finally, there are circumstances where the Official Solicitor is invited by the court on this type of application to attend as amicus curiae. An ordinarily competent adult, for example, may be refusing medical treatment, which doctors feel is not only necessary but vital to the patient's well-being, yet the patient may be willing or capable of instructing solicitors. This type of case may come on very urgently before the court, with the patient and NHS Trust or health authority represented. The court, however, may wish the assistance of the Official Solicitor as an amicus curiae in relation to expert evidence, any other urgent enquiries requiring to be made and guidance as to the options for disposal of the case. The role of the Official Solicitor then will be to assist the court as far as he can. In *Re MB (Medical Treatment)* [1997] 2 FLR 426, the patient was withholding her consent to medical treatment because of her needle phobia. There, for example, the Official Solicitor was invited to attend and act as amicus curiae for the benefit of the court.

Part II

SPECIFIC AREAS IN RELATION TO MEDICAL TREATMENT AND THE LAW

Chapter 5

THE WITHHOLDING OR WITHDRAWAL OF LIFE-SUSTAINING TREATMENT IN RELATION TO ADULTS AND MINORS

5.1 PRELIMINARY PRINCIPLES

In any case where a court is invited to authorise some step which may lead to the withdrawal of life-sustaining treatment and whatever the category, there are three preliminary basic principles.

(i) The court's high respect for the sanctity of human life imposes a strong presumption in favour of taking all steps capable of preserving it, save in exceptional circumstances.

(ii) The test to be applied is whether the medical treatment the patient is receiving or may receive is in his or her best interests. In this regard, the test is the same whether the court is concerned with a minor or an incompetent adult: *Re R (Adult: Medical Treatment)* [1996] 2 FLR 99 at 108B and *Airedale NHS Trust v Bland* [1993] AC 789, CA at 820C. The jurisdiction the court has, however, is different as between the two. The parens patriae jurisdiction is applicable in relation to minors, while the court may, in its inherent jurisdiction in relation to incompetent adults, declare whether proposed medical treatment is lawful as being in a patient's best interests.

(iii) The court never sanctions steps to terminate life which would be unlawful. There is no question of approving a course aimed at terminating life or accelerating death. The court is concerned only with the circumstances in which steps should not be taken to prolong life.

These three preliminary or basic principles are set out by Taylor LJ in a case concerning a child: *Re J (A Minor) (Wardship: Medical Treatment)* [1991] 1 FLR 366 at 381 and confirmed, in relation to relevant cases involving adults, by Sir Stephen Brown, the President, in *Re R (Adult: Medical Treatment)* [1996] 2 FLR 99 at 107B and in *Re H (A Patient)* [1998] 2 FLR 36 at 40C–40H.

It is also generally to be noted that the BMA has issued from its Medical Ethics Committee a consultation paper entitled 'Withdrawing and Withholding Treatment', whose purpose is to consider reviewing the approach to this field of medical practice.

5.2   THE DEFINITION OF DEATH

Part III of this book includes a review paper by a working group convened by the Royal College of Physicians entitled 'Criteria for the Diagnosis of Brain-Stem Death'. It is set out in the *Journal of the Royal College of Physicians of London* vol 29, no 5, September/October 1995, p 381. It is there suggested that 'irreversible loss of the capacity for consciousness, combined with the irreversible loss of the capacity to breathe' should be regarded as the definition of death. It continues:

> 'The irreversible cessation of brain stem function [brain stem death] ... will produce the forementioned clinical state and therefore brain stem death is equivalent to the death of the individual. It is suggested that the more correct term "brain stem death" should replace the term brain death ...'

5.3   TWO CATEGORIES OF CASE

There are two categories of case in this area, described by Lord Goff in the case of *Airedale NHS Trust v Bland* [1993] AC 789, HL at 868–869. The first is where, having regard to all the circumstances (including, for example, the intrusive nature of the treatment, the hazards involved in it and the very poor quality of life which may be prolonged for the patient if the treatment is successful), it may be judged not to be in the best interests of the patient to initiate or continue life-prolonging treatment. This category of case extends to those who are profoundly handicapped, usually with severe brain damage. The other is where, so far as the living patient is concerned, the treatment is of no benefit to him because he is totally unconscious and there is no prospect of any improvement in his condition, particularly those patients in PVS (the permanent vegetative state). In both classes of case, the decision whether or not to withhold or withdraw treatment must be made in the best interests of the patient. In the first category of case discussed, the decision has to be made by weighing the relevant considerations. In the second category of case there is, as set out by Lord Goff at p 869, in reality no weighing operation. Both categories of case and the approach to be taken in relation to them are scrutinised in detail in this chapter.

5.4   PVS (THE PERMANENT VEGETATIVE STATE)

5.4.1   The meaning and definition of PVS

Professor Bryan Jennett and Professor Plum coined the term 'PVS' in 1972. It describes the syndrome that was being increasingly encountered as the life-saving and life-sustaining technologies of intensive care were securing the survival of some patients with brain damage of a severity that would previously have proved fatal.

PVS is a recognised medical condition, quite distinct from other conditions sometimes known as 'irreversible coma', 'the Guillain-Barré syndrome', 'the locked-in syndrome' and 'brain death'. In PVS, the cortex, that part of the brain which is the seat of cognitive function and sensory capacity, is destroyed through prolonged deprivation of oxygen. The cortex resolves into a watery mass. The consciousness which is the central feature of individual personality departs forever. However, the brain stem, which controls the reflexive functions of the body, in particular heartbeat, breathing and digestion, continues to operate. In the eyes of the medical world and of the law, a person is not clinically dead so long as the brain stem retains its function, ie the PVS patient continues to breathe unaided and his digestion continues to function. However, although his eyes are open, he cannot see or hear; although capable of reflex movement, particularly in response to painful stimuli, the patient is incapable of voluntary movement and can feel no pain; he cannot taste or smell; he cannot speak or communicate in any way; he has no cognitive function and can thus feel no emotion, whether pleasure or distress. A common feature of the vegetative patient is that, after a variable time in coma, wakefulness returns with long periods of spontaneous eye opening.

In Part III of this book, there is enclosed the Review by a Working Group convened by the Royal College of Physicians entitled the 'Permanent Vegetative State'. It is set out in the *Journal of the Royal College of Physicians of London* vol 30, no 2, March/April 1996, p 119. The Review states that the condition is to be known as the permanent vegetative state, as opposed to the persistent vegetative state. It covers wide-ranging guidance to the medical profession on the condition, including the definition of PVS and the criteria for diagnosis. The last page of the Review sets out a table, indicating the distinguishing factors between PVS, coma, locked-in syndrome and brain stem death. The Review also specifies the three clinical criteria which must all be fulfilled for the diagnosis to be considered. First, there shall be no evidence of awareness of self or environment at any time. There shall be no volitional response to visual, auditory, tactile or noxious stimuli. There shall be no evidence of language comprehension or expression. Secondly, there shall be the presence of cycles of eye closure and eye opening which may simulate sleep and waking. Thirdly, there shall be sufficiently preserved hypothalamic and brain stem function to ensure the maintenance of respiration and circulation. The view of the Working Group is that a diagnosis of PVS may reasonably be made when a patient has been in a continuing vegetative state following head injury for more than 12 months or following other causes of brain damage for more than six months.

It is also helpful in this regard to read the analysis by Sir Stephen Brown, President of the Family Division, of the medical evidence presented to him at first instance in the *Bland* case, including that of Professor Jennett in relation to the distinguishing factors between PVS and coma, locked-in syndrome and brain stem death.

5.4.2   The case of *Airedale NHS Trust v Bland* [1993] AC 789

The significance of the case

The case raised for the first time in the English courts the following question: in what circumstances, if any, can a doctor lawfully discontinue life-sustaining treatment, including nutrition and hydration, without which a patient will die? At issue in the case was whether, as was advised by the hospital where Anthony Bland was cared for, a declaration should be granted that it was lawful to discontinue the artificial feeding and supply of antibiotics to him, with the result that, inevitably, within about one or two weeks, he would die. Sir Thomas Bingham MR in the Court of Appeal put the matter to be as whether artificial feeding and antibiotics drugs might lawfully be withheld or withdrawn from an insensate patient with no hope of recovery when it was known that, if that was done, the patient would shortly thereafter die. The judgments at first instance, in the Court of Appeal and in the House of Lords, raise and embrace wide-ranging issues involving principles of law, morality, ethics and medical practice.

The facts

Anthony Bland, who was then 17 years old, was present at the football match at Hillsborough in Sheffield where, owing to the failure of crowd control, a number of people in the crowd were crushed. Tragically many were killed. He suffered serious injuries and, as a result of them, the supply of oxygen to his brain was interrupted. He suffered catastrophic and irremediable damage to his brain. His condition was that of PVS; the space which the cortex of his brain should have occupied was filled with watery fluid. He had been a PVS patient for more than two and a half years by the time his case came before the court and the evidence was that he could have continued to live for many years longer. Because he could still breathe, he did not need the assistance of a respirator. He was fed by means of a tube, threaded through his nose and down into his stomach, through which liquefied food was mechanically pumped; his bowels were evacuated by enema; his bladder was drained by catheter. He was subject to repeated bouts of infection affecting his urinary tract and chest. He was, on the evidence, totally insensate. After careful thought, his family agreed that the feeding tubes should be removed.

The relief sought

With the agreement of Mr Bland's family, as well as the consultant in charge of his case, and the support of two independent doctors, the Airedale NHS Trust, as plaintiffs in the action, applied by originating summons to the Family Division of the High Court for declarations that they might lawfully discontinue all life-sustaining treatment and medical support measures designed to keep him alive, including the termination of ventilation, nutrition and hydration by artificial means. A declaration was further sought that they might lawfully discontinue, and thereafter need not furnish, medical treatment to him, except for the sole purpose of enabling him to end his life and die peacefully with the greatest dignity and the least pain, suffering and distress.

The reasoning for the decision by the House of Lords

(a) Omission as opposed to positive act

English criminal law draws a sharp distinction between acts and omissions. If an act resulting in death is done without lawful excuse and with intent to kill, it is murder. However, an omission to act with the same result and with the same intent is, in general, not an offence at all. To the latter general principle there is the exception at common law that a person may be criminally liable for the consequences of an omission if he stands in such a relation to the victim that he is under a duty to act. It was held by the House of Lords in the *Bland* case that the cessation of artificial nutrition and hydration was an omission, not an act. Accordingly, such cessation of treatment amounted to the doctor simply allowing his patient to die of his pre-existing condition (per Lord Goff at p 866):

> 'I agree that the doctor's conduct in discontinuing life support can properly be categorised as an omission. It is true that it may be difficult to describe what the doctor actually does as an omission, for example where he takes some positive step to bring the life support to an end. But discontinuation of life support is, for present purposes, no different from not initiating life support in the first place. In each case, the doctor is simply allowing his patient to die in the sense that he is desisting from taking a step which might in certain circumstances prevent his patient from dying as a result of his pre-existing condition: and as a matter of general principle an omission such as this, will not be unlawful unless it constitutes a breach of duty to the patient.'

In drawing a distinction between acts and omissions the law forbids the taking of active measures to cut short the life of a terminally ill patient. Lord Goff, in seeking to describe the difference, in legal consequences, between the doctor discontinuing life support as against him or her ending a patient's life by a lethal injection, went on to say at p 866:

> '. . . But in the end the reason for that difference is that, whereas the law considers that discontinuance of life support may be consistent with the doctor's duty to care for his patient, it does not, for reasons of policy, consider that it forms any part of his duty to give his patient a lethal injection to put him out of his agony.'

(b) The duty or right, if any, of a doctor to treat where treatment is futile and of no benefit

Having reached the view that the withdrawal of treatment would amount to an omission, not an act, the court then had to consider whether, notwithstanding such omission, the doctors were, or were not, still under a continuing duty to treat Anthony Bland. The cessation or withdrawal of treatment would not be a criminal act unless the doctors were under a duty to continue the regime of treatment.

It is appropriate to emphasise that Anthony Bland had never been able to consent to or refuse the treatment given to him. He had left no advance statement or 'living will' as to his wishes and feelings. Accordingly, he could only be treated in the absence of his consent as permitted by the common law. The principles of *Re F (Sterilisation: Mental Patient)* [1990] 2 AC 1, in those circumstances, were viewed to be applicable to Anthony Bland by the House of Lords, namely that a doctor is under a duty to treat a patient who is incapable of consenting, provided that the treatment concerned is in the best interests of such a patient. However, a doctor's decision whether invasive care is in the best interests of the patient falls to be assessed by reference to the test laid down in *Bolam v Friern Hospital Management Committee* [1957] 1 WLR 582. The test is whether a decision as to medical treatment is in accordance with a practice accepted at the time by a responsible body of medical opinion.

The doctors into whose charge Anthony Bland originally came made decisions about his care and treatment which he could not make for himself. Those decisions were made in line with the principles of *Re F* in his best interests. Throughout the period when the possibility still existed that he might recover, his best interests justified the application of the necessary life support system without his consent.

The agreed medical evidence was that no benefit at all would be conferred by continuance of the treatment, given that he was totally insensate, with no hope of recovery.

In the light of the test set out in the case of *Re F*, accordingly, it was held by the House of Lords in the *Bland* case that the doctors could be under no duty to continue to treat Anthony Bland when they, the medical practitioners, felt such treatment which could be of no benefit to him, was not in his best interests. Lord Keith of Kinkel, at pp 858 and 859, said:

> '... a medical practitioner is under no duty to continue to treat such a patient where a large body of informed and responsible medical opinion is to the effect that no benefit at all would be conferred by continuance. Existence in a vegetative state with no prospect of recovery is by that opinion regarded as not being a benefit, and that ... at least forms a proper basis for the decision to discontinue treatment and care: *Bolam v Friern Hospital Management Committee* [1957] 1 WLR 582.'

Lord Browne-Wilkinson went further, in taking the view that there could be no question of the doctors being under a duty to treat him, since their original right to treat had now gone (at pp 883–884):

> 'In my judgment it must follow from this that if there comes a stage where the responsible doctor comes to the reasonable conclusion (which accords with the views of a responsible body of medical opinion) that further continuance of an intrusive life support system is not in the best interests of the patient, he can no longer lawfully continue that life support system: to do so would constitute the crime of battery and the tort of trespass to the person. Therefore he cannot be in breach of any duty to maintain the patient's life.'

It is not possible to do justice to the wide variety of issues raised in the *Bland* case, nor to the differing emphases of the varying judges in their judgments from first instance through to the House of Lords. It suffices to note what Lord Goff said at p 869:

'But in the end, in a case such as the present, it is the futility of the treatment which justifies its termination. I do not consider that, in circumstances such as these, a doctor is required to initiate or to continue life-prolonging treatment or care in the best interests of his patient. It follows that no such duty rests upon the respondents, or upon Dr H, in the case of Anthony Bland, whose condition is in reality no more than a living death, and for whom such treatment or care would, in medical terms, be futile.'

5.4.3   The sanctity of life: the duty to prolong life

The fundamental principle of the sanctity of life is not absolute and may yield to other factors, in exceptional circumstances. A doctor caring for a patient is not under an absolute obligation to prolong the patient's life by any means available to him or her, regardless of the circumstances and the quality of the patient's life.

A doctor who has under his or her care a patient suffering painfully from terminal cancer cannot be under an absolute obligation to perform upon such a patient major surgery to abate another condition which, if unabated, would, or might, shorten his life still further: *Auckland Area Health Board v The Attorney-General* [1993] 1 NZLR 235 at 253.

The principle of the sanctity of life does not compel a doctor to treat a patient of sound mind who will die if he does not, contrary to the express wishes of the patient. It does not authorise similarly forcible feeding of prisoners of sound mind who are on, for whatever reason, hunger strike. Nor does it compel the temporary keeping alive of patients who are terminally ill, where to do so would merely prolong their suffering. The principle of the sanctity of life would, however, prohibit as unlawful the taking of active measures to cut short the life of a terminally ill patient: see *Airedale NHS Trust v Bland* [1993] AC 789 at 859.

5.4.4   Opposition to the withholding or withdrawing of life-sustaining treatment by family

In the case of *Re G (Persistent Vegetative State)* [1995] 2 FCR 46, a married man, then aged 24, was involved in a serious motorcycle accident. He suffered head injuries that resulted in him becoming unconscious. Subsequently, he suffered a cardiac arrest that interrupted the flow of blood to his brain and he sustained further brain damage. He never regained consciousness, and in December 1992, some 18 months after the accident, he was diagnosed as being in a persistent vegetative state. All the medical evidence supported this view. G received artificial nutrition and hydration through a gastrostomy tube. In June 1993, Mr J, the consultant orthopaedic surgeon who had the care of G, discussed the future care of G with his wife. She indicated that she considered it not to be in his best interests to continue the artificial hydration and nutrition. The doctor agreed. The patient's mother, however, disagreed and wished it to continue. The Hospital Trust where G was cared for sought declarations from the court that would permit the withdrawal of feeding and which would inevitably lead to G's death. The Official Solicitor representing G supported the Hospital Trust's application. The patient's mother was a party to the originating summons, which was issued on 16

February 1994, seeking the declaratory relief referred to. It was submitted on behalf of the mother that her opposition should operate as a veto. This argument was rejected by the court. The approach taken by the court was consistent with the guidelines of the BMA on treatment decisions for patients in the permanent vegetative state, para 5 of which reads:

> 'It is good practice for doctors to consult the wishes of people close to the patient but their views alone cannot determine the treatment of the PVS patient. People close to the patient may be able to throw light on the wishes of the PVS patient regarding the prolongation of treatment and this is likely to be helpful in decision making. Treatment decisions, however, must be based upon the doctors' assessment of the patients' best interests.'

Whilst it is good practice, accordingly, to consult the wishes and feelings of those close to the patient in relation to treatment, the decision is for the doctor and his or her team who have responsibility for the care of the patient. As a matter of law, the next of kin of the patient has no legal right either to consent or to refuse consent on behalf of the patient: *Re T (An Adult) (Consent to Medical Treatment)* [1992] 2 FLR 458 at 461B, per Lord Donaldson MR. This is reflected at para 2.5 of the consultation paper 'Withdrawing and Withholding Treatment' from the BMA's Medical Ethics Committee.

Both Lord Donaldson's dicta in *Re T* and para 2.5 of the consultation paper indicate that the importance of consulting with close family and/or next of kin may lie in revealing or throwing light on the wishes of the PVS patient himself or herself. As may be seen from Chapter 9 on Advance Statements or 'living wills', those responsible for the patient's care must take account of and respect the patient's own views, when known, whether these are formally recorded in a written document (an advance refusal or advance directive) or not. Such a duty by a doctor to his or her patient is envisaged and reflected at p 121 of the Review Paper headed 'The Permanent Vegetative State' of the Working Group convened by the Royal College of Physicians: *Journal of the Royal College of Physicians of London* vol 30, no 2, March/April 1996, p 119. This Review Paper is reproduced in Part III of this book. The importance of the view of the patient is also to be seen in para 10 of the Official Solicitor's Practice Note on PVS of 26 July 1996 [1996] 3 FLR 606.

In *Re G*, the court held that it would be an appalling burden to place on any relative the responsibility of making a decision in such a grave case. Relief was granted by the court, notwithstanding the patient's mother's objections.

In a case involving a critically ill minor – not a PVS case – *Re J (A Minor) (Wardship: Medical Treatment)* [1991] 1 FLR 366 at 381, Taylor LJ said:

> '... the views of the parents, although they should be heeded and weighed, cannot prevail over the court's view of the ward's best interests.'

5.4.5 Urgent applications in relation to the withholding or withdrawing of life-sustaining treatment

In the case of *Frenchay Healthcare NHS Trust v S* [1994] 1 FLR 485, the patient suffered acute brain damage in June 1991 after taking an overdose of drugs. In October 1991, he was transferred to a rehabilitation unit. The consultant in charge of his case, who had extensive experience of the treatment of the acutely disabled, diagnosed the patient as being in a persistent vegetative state. He required constant and intensive nursing and was fed through a nasogastric tube until June 1993, when that method of feeding having become impracticable, an operation was performed to insert a gastronomy tube through the stomach wall. On 10 January 1994 the tube became dislodged so that it was impossible to feed the patient at all. The consultant took the view that the further surgical procedure required to insert another tube would be against the patient's interests, that since there was no possibility of improvement he should be allowed to die naturally, and that if the tube were not reinstated the process of dying could not cause him distress. Accordingly, as a matter of urgency, the plaintiff Hospital Trust obtained from the judge a declaration authorising the Trust not to replace the tube. The Official Solicitor appealed on behalf of the patient on the basis, applying the principles set out in *Airedale NHS Trust v Bland*, first, that the hurried procedure adopted had deprived the patient of a fair and full exploration of the issues and, secondly, that the medical opinions before the court as to whether the patient was in a permanent vegetative state were not unanimous. The Court of Appeal rejected the contention that there had been no opportunity for there to be a full exploration of the facts which, in other circumstances, would have been desirable. Emergency situations, they held, were bound to arise where it was impracticable for the court to consider a case in such a way, or even for the plaintiff to apply to the court at all. In relation to the second point raised, on the medical evidence, they determined that the patient was in a permanent vegetative state, that there was no prospect of recovery and that he had no cognitive function worth the name. That being the case, it was not right, in the acute emergency which had arisen, for the court to attach great weight to the points of distinction raised between the case in question and that of *Airedale NHS Trust v Bland*. It was for the court to decide what was in the patient's best interests in the light of the doctors' opinions and of all the facts. The appeal was dismissed.

In the case of *Re D (Medical Treatment)* [1998] 1 FLR 411, the court was concerned with a young woman in PVS. The tube which was responsible for feeding her by the gastrostomy process became detached and fell out of its position, creating an emergency situation. Temporary sustenance was provided by intravenous means, a method which could not continue for long. This prompted the Hospital Trust to issue an application for declarations that it would be lawful in the circumstances of M's medical condition to withdraw the artificial feeding and hydration which was keeping her body alive. The hospital had already been considering such a course. Nevertheless, the matter came on for hearing very quickly with full medical evidence and representation of the patient through her guardian ad litem, the Official Solicitor, and of the Trust.

5.4.6 PVS cases where a clinical feature of the condition is absent

In two separate cases, namely in *Re D (Medical Treatment)* [1998] 1 FLR 411 and *Re H (A Patient)* [1998] 2 FLR 36, the court considered the guidelines on PVS issued by the Royal College of Physicians.

Whilst, in each case, the mandatory three clinical requirements were met in relation to diagnosis of PVS, other clinical features are referred to in the guidelines including 'there will not be nystagmus in response to ice water caloric testing, the patient will not have visual fixation, be able to track moving objects with the eyes or show a "menace response".'

In *Re D* at p 418H, it was found that the patient was able to track movements with the eyes and show a menace response and there was nystagmus in response to ice water caloric testing. In *Re H*, referred to above, there was evidence again of visual tracking.

In both cases, although the patients did not fit four squarely with one particular guideline, they were each in a state of PVS: neither had any degree of awareness whatsoever; neither was susceptible, on the evidence, to any change; each patient was in a state falling within the description of a 'living death'. In neither case was there any evidence of any meaningful life.

It is perhaps obvious to say that, in any case of suggested PVS, the court will wish to scrutinise the evidence carefully to ensure that the condition of PVS is established: *Swindon and Marlborough NHS Trust v S* [1995] Med LR 84.

5.4.7 Practice and procedure in PVS cases

In *Airedale NHS Trust v Bland* [1993] AC 789 at 873, Lord Goff confirmed the view of the President, Sir Stephen Brown, that the opinion of the court should be sought in all cases similar to that of Anthony Bland 'for the protection of patients and doctors and the reassurance of the patients' families and the public'. He further agreed that, in the course of time, a body of experience and practice will build up which will obviate the need for applications in every such case.

The practice and procedure is set out in the Practice Note on PVS of the Official Solicitor of 26 July 1996 [1996] 2 FLR 375, which is reproduced in Part III of this book. Practitioners should consider the full terms and effects of such Practice Note.

The termination of artificial feeding and hydration of patients in PVS will, in virtually all cases, require the prior sanction of a High Court judge.

Applications to the court should be by originating summons, issued in the Family Division of the High Court seeking declaratory relief. The application must be supported by affidavit and medical evidence.

The applicants may be either the next of kin or the relevant Health Authority or Trust (which, in any event, ought to be a party).

The Official Solicitor should be invited to act as guardian ad litem of the respondent, who will inevitably be a patient within the meaning of RSC, Ord 80. In these cases, the patient will not be able, of course, to speak or act for himself or herself.

There should be at least two neurological reports on the patient, one of which will be commissioned by the Official Solicitor.

Any views of the patient previously expressed, either in writing or otherwise, will be an important component in the court's decision. The views of next of kin are also important and should be made known to the court.

Applications to the court in relation to minors should be made within wardship proceedings. In such cases, the applicant should seek leave of the court for the termination of feeding and hydration, rather than a declaration. The form of relief set out below in relation to adult patients should be amended accordingly.

The originating summons should seek, in relation to patients who are adults, relief in the following form:

> 'It is declared that despite the inability of X to give a valid consent, the plaintiff and/or the responsible medical practitioners:
>
> (i)   may lawfully discontinue all life-sustaining treatment and medical support measures designed to keep X alive in his or her existing permanent vegetative state including the termination of ventilation, nutrition and hydration by artificial means and
> (ii) may lawfully discontinue and thereafter need not furnish medical treatment to X except for the sole purpose of enabling X to end his or her life and to die peacefully with the greatest dignity and the least distress.
>
> It is ordered that in the event of a material change in the existing circumstances occurring before the withdrawal of artificial feeding and hydration any party shall have liberty to apply for such further or other declaration or order as may be just.'

Whilst the court has jurisdiction to decide whether or not a hearing, or part of a hearing, is to be in Chambers or in open court, normally that discretion will be exercised in favour of those cases being heard in public: *Re G (Adult Patient: Publicity)* [1995] 2 FLR 528. The latter was a case concerning a PVS patient, where the President of the Family Division, Sir Stephen Brown, in directing that the substantive hearing would be in open court, said that the issue to be considered was a 'matter of life and death'. Accordingly, the case will normally be in open court. The court will, however, usually take steps to preserve the anonymity of the patient and the patient's family and, where appropriate, the hospital, by making orders under s 11 of the Contempt of Court Act 1981. An order restricting publicity will continue to have effect, notwithstanding the death of the patient, unless and until an application is made to discharge it: *Re C (Adult Patient: Publicity)* [1996] 2 FLR 251.

One exception in relation to such cases being heard in public is where the court is exercising its parens patriae jurisdiction and, in such cases involving minors, a hearing in Chambers with judgment in open court (subject of course to preserving anonymity) may be the appropriate course as per the dicta in *Re C (A Minor) (Wardship: Medical Treatment)* [1990] Fam 26 at 37E.

5.5   THE WITHHOLDING OR WITHDRAWAL OF LIFE-SUSTAINING TREATMENT FOR THOSE CRITICALLY ILL ADULTS OR MINORS, OTHER THAN THOSE IN PVS

5.5.1   Adults

CPR (cardio-pulmonary resuscitation)
Cardio-pulmonary resuscitation (CPR) can be attempted on any individual in whom cardiac or respiratory function ceases. The medical profession was concerned to consider in what circumstances CPR might be inappropriate. In March 1993, the BMA and the Royal College of Nursing published a joint statement entitled 'Decisions relating to CPR: a statement from the BMA and the RCN in association with the Resuscitation Council (UK)'. Within this statement are guidelines issued for the medical profession, and a copy of the joint statement is reproduced in Part III of this book.

DNR (do-not-resuscitate) decisions
Paragraph 1 of the guidelines in the joint statement referred to above is as follows:

> 'It is appropriate to consider a do-not-resuscitate (DNR) decision in the following circumstances:
>
> a.   where the patient's condition indicates that effective cardio-pulmonary resuscitation (CPR) is unlikely to be successful.
> b.   where CPR is not in accord with the recorded, sustained wishes of the patient who is mentally competent.
> c.   where successful CPR is likely to be followed by a length and quality of life which would not be acceptable to the patient.'

It is important to emphasise the word 'decision' in relation to DNR, since anything amounting to a policy to not resuscitate within a hospital would be questionable. The circumstances of each individual patient for whom the consideration arises must be considered, and the overall responsibility for a DNR decision must rest with the consultant in charge of the patient's care. It will invariably be the case that the consultant will discuss the circumstances with others in his or her medical team. It may also be possible for the patient's wishes to be explored, for example, those who are at risk of cardiac or respiratory failure or who have terminal illness.

In para 9 of the guidelines, it is emphasised that, if a DNR decision is based on quality of life considerations, the views of the patient, where these can be ascertained, are particularly important. If a patient cannot express a view, the opinion of the family, or others close to the patient, may be sought regarding the patient's best interests.

Re R (Adult: Medical Treatment) [1996] 2 FLR 99

R, a 23-year-old adult, was born with a serious malfunction of the brain and cerebral palsy. He was not in the category of someone in a permanent vegetative state, but his state of awareness rated between one and two on the scale of ten. He had developed severe epilepsy. He was believed to be deaf and blind. He could not chew and food had to be syringed to the back of his mouth. He suffered from thrush and had ulcers, all the way through to his guts. He was able to give an indication of pleasure when cuddled. He responded to pain and was able to grimace. He was living in a residential home and the manager of that home was of the view that he had never worked with anyone so physically or mentally handicapped as R.

In 1995, R was admitted to hospital on five occasions, suffering from recurrent chest infections, severe constipation, bleeding from ulceration, fits, and dehydration and under-nutrition.

After his fifth distressing hospital admission, Dr Andrew, the doctor concerned, and the parents agreed that if, in future, R should suffer a life-threatening condition involving a cardiac arrest, he should not be subjected to cardio-pulmonary resuscitation.

Accordingly, on 22 September 1995, the consultant in question signed an NHS Trust direction headed 'Do not resuscitate', giving the name of R, his date of birth, followed by these words: 'It is agreed that cardio-pulmonary resuscitation is not to be given to the above named person'. Under the heading 'next of kin', the patient's mother's signature appeared, then the consultant's signature and also the signature of the home manager.

Certain members of the instructor staff at the day-care centre which R attended objected to the DNR notice. It was made clear by the consultant that there was no question of 'a no treatment policy'. The DNR notice referred only to the question of CPR.

Having heard evidence, the judge was satisfied that, if CPR was attempted, it would be a dangerous operation, having regard to R's frailty, and, indeed, might cause him to suffer further brain damage.

Dr Andrew's evidence to the court was that, even in hospital settings, on average about 13 per cent of patients receiving CPR survived to discharge. In a residential home, such as the one R lived in, without medical staff present, the chances of a successful resuscitation would be almost nil.

Referring back to para 1 of the guidelines of the joint statement, in the case of R it was point (a) which appeared to be particularly relevant, namely that CPR was unlikely to be effective or successful (*Re R (Adult: Medical Treatment)* [1996] 2 FLR 99 at 106A).

Practice and procedure

In the case of *Re R*, an application for leave to apply for judicial review was issued on behalf of R himself by a 'next friend', seeking an order for certiorari to quash the Trust's DNR notice. Leave to apply for judicial review was granted and the judicial review was adjourned to be heard with the action of the NHS Trust, which issued an originating summons in the Family Division of the High Court seeking declarations in various terms.

At the hearing, the Official Solicitor acted as guardian ad litem for the patient R, the Trust was represented and the parents appeared in person.

It is helpful to set out the terms of the judge's order in the case of *Re R*, set out at p 109 of the judgment. The court ordered and declared that:

'notwithstanding:
(a) that the patient is unable to give a valid consent thereto; and
(b) if such be the case that no further order of the court shall have been obtained in the meantime,
it shall be lawful as being in the patient's best interests for the trust and/the responsible medical practitioners having the responsibility at the time for the patient's treatment and care:
(1) to perform the said proposed gastrostomy;
(2) to withhold cardio-pulmonary resuscitation of the patient;
(3) to withhold the administration of antibiotics in the event of the patient developing a potentially life-threatening infection which would otherwise call for the administration of antibiotics but only if immediately prior to withholding the same:
    (a) the trust is so advised both by the general medical practitioner and by the consultant psychiatrist having the responsibility at the time for the patient's treatment and case; and
    (b) one or other or both of the parents first give their consent thereto;
(4) generally to furnish such treatment and nursing care as may from time to time be appropriate to ensure that the patient suffers the least distress and retains the greatest dignity.'

Restricting the publication of details of the patient and his family

The court will usually take steps to preserve the anonymity of the patient and the patient's family by making appropriate orders under the Contempt of Court Act 1981 (*Re G (Adult Patient: Publicity)* [1995] 2 FLR 528). The court has jurisdiction to decide whether or not the hearing shall be in Chambers or in open court.

Following the reasoning of the President in *Re G*, there would appear to be no reason why, within the court's discretion, non-PVS cases in relation to the medical treatment of adults should not be considered to be heard in public, where the circumstances and gravity are akin to that of a PVS case and involve any question of the withdrawal of life-sustaining medical treatment whether immediately or contingently in the future.

Adult patients who are unable to co-operate with medical treatment such that it cannot be effected

Circumstances have arisen where a patient has been in need of medical treatment for a serious condition and the hospital has sought to treat the patient accordingly, yet the patient has been unwilling to co-operate with the required programme of treatment. It is necessary to compare and contrast two cases in this regard.

In *Re D (Medical Treatment: Mentally Disabled Patient)* [1998] 2 FLR 22, the patient D was a man of 49 years who had spent a large part of his life in and out of psychiatric hospitals. Within the appropriate test as to competence, he lacked the capacity to consent to or refuse treatment. He had developed a serious kidney complaint and required dialysis three to four times a week, for periods of up to four hours. He was unable to co-operate consistently with the treatment, and the only way in which dialysis could be carried out was to place D under a general anaesthetic each time, which was dangerous and impractical. The hospital authority sought the protection of the court in the form of a declaration that it was lawful for them not to impose treatment on D in the likely event that they continued to be unable to treat him. D was represented by the Official Solicitor.

A declaration, accordingly, was granted by the court in the following terms:

> '... that, notwithstanding the defendant's inability to consent to or refuse medical treatment, it is lawful as being in the best interests of the patient for the plaintiff ... not to impose haemodialysis upon him in circumstances in which, in the opinion of the medical practitioners responsible for such treatment, it is not reasonably practicable so to do.'

In the case of *Re JT (Adult: Refusal of Medical Treatment)* [1998] 1 FLR 48, in similar circumstances, the two NHS Trusts involved issued an originating summons seeking declarations that, although the patient was capable of refusing medical treatment, it would be lawful for the two Trusts not to perform renal dialysis upon her. The patient was a 25-year-old woman who resided in a hospital, suffering from mental disability, and had developed renal failure.

Several attempts were made, unsuccessfully, to give her renal dialysis but eventually the patient refused further medical treatment, expressing instead her desire to die. Whereas in *Re D* (above) the patient lacked capacity, in the case of *Re JT*, the judge applied the three-stage test as to capacity laid down by Thorpe J, as he then was, in *Re C* [1994] 1 All ER 819 and it was clear on the evidence that the young woman was capable of all three stages of that test. Accordingly, she had the capacity to refuse treatment, and the Trusts were bound by that refusal, since, if they imposed dialysis against her will, they would be committing a criminal and tortious act. In these circumstances, the court held that it was unnecessary for the court to grant a declaration that the withholding of such treatment was lawful. The originating summons was dismissed. Because of the patient's competence, there was no need to appoint the Official Solicitor as her guardian ad litem, and she was represented by her own solicitor and counsel, as were the two Trusts.

5.5.2   Minors

A framework for practice
In September 1997, the Royal College of Paediatrics and Child Health issued a Framework for Practice in relation to withholding or withdrawing life-saving treatment on children. It is an important document which provides a framework for medical practitioners in relation to their approach towards withholding or withdrawing treatment from a child. It was the result of two years' research and covers a wide range of issues and guidance in relation to the approach to be taken in varying circumstances by practitioners.

Set out on p 7 of the Framework there is a summary, as set out below.

There are five situations where the withholding or withdrawal of curative medical treatment might be considered:

'(1)   The brain dead child. In the older child, where criteria of brain stem death are agreed by two practitioners in the usual way, it may still be technically feasible to provide basic cardio-respiratory support by means of ventilation and intensive care. It is agreed within the profession that treatment in such circumstances is futile and the withdrawal of current medical treatment is appropriate.

(2)   The permanent vegetative state. The child who develops a permanent vegetative state following insults, such as trauma or hypoxia, is reliant on others for all care and does not react to or relate with the outside world. It may be appropriate both to withdraw current therapy and to withhold further curative treatment.

(3)   The 'no chance' situation. The child has such severe disease that life-sustaining treatment simply delays death without significant alleviation of suffering. Medical treatment in this situation may thus be deemed inappropriate.

(4)   The 'no purpose' situation. Although the patient may be able to survive with treatment, the degree of physical or mental impairment will be so great that it is unreasonable to expect them to bear it. The child in this situation will never be capable of taking part in decisions regarding treatment or its withdrawal.

(5)   The 'unbearable' situation. The child and/or family feel that, in the face of progressive and irreversible illness, further treatment is more than can be borne. They wish to have a particular treatment withdrawn or to refuse further treatment, irrespective of the medical opinion on its potential benefit. Oncology patients who are offered further aggressive treatment might be included in this category.'

The test for the courts

There is only one test and that is that the court's prime and paramount consideration must be the best interests of the child. The court will weigh and test all the evidence and reach a decision according to the child's best interests.

Parens patriae

Unlike the position in relation to adults who lack capacity, the court may, in relation to minors, exercise the parens patriae jurisdiction, thereby taking over the rights and duties of the parents. This is not to say that the parents will be excluded from the decision-making process. However, in the end, the responsibility for the decision, whether to give or to withhold consent, is that of the court alone.

In relation to minors, the court is able to consent or not consent, as the case may be, for and on behalf of the child to any proposed medical treatment.

Minors who are severely handicapped but not dying

In *Re J (A Minor) (Wardship: Medical Treatment)* [1991] 1 FLR 366, the Official Solicitor asked the court for guidance as to the proper approach with regard to children who were severely handicapped but not dying. The submission of the Official Solicitor was that, aside from the case of a child who is already terminally ill, there was an absolute rule that the court was never justified in withholding consent to treatment which would enable a child to survive a life-threatening condition, whatever the pain or the side effects inherent in the treatment and whatever the quality of life which it would experience thereafter.

The child was born in May 1990, prematurely, weighing only two and a half pounds. Due to shortage of oxygen and impaired blood supply, the little boy suffered severe brain damage. There were recurrent convulsions and episodes where he stopped breathing and, as a result, he spent two periods of six weeks on a ventilator. The child was not dying or on the point of death. The most optimistic view was that he would develop spastic quadriplegia, that he was likely to be blind and deaf and that he would never be able to speak or develop even limited intellectual abilities.

The child was made a ward of court. The question arose as to whether the court should approve what was proposed by the doctors. The fundamental medical issue was whether, if the child suffered another collapse and stopped breathing, he should be put back on a mechanical ventilator. On the evidence, the doctors were unanimous that, in his present condition, Baby J should not be put back on to such a mechanical ventilator. Three factors stood out. First, the severe lack of capacity of the child in all his faculties, which, even without any further complication, would make his existence barely sentient. Secondly, further mechanical ventilation, if required, would itself involve the risk of a deterioration in the child's condition and of further brain damage. Thirdly, all the doctors drew attention to the invasive and distressing nature of mechanical ventilation and the intensive care required to accompany it.

The Court of Appeal endorsed the judge's decision at first instance, approving the medical recommendations and holding that it would not be in the child's best interests to subject him to a mechanical ventilator if he stopped breathing, whilst at the same time leaving the doctors free to take more active measures to preserve the child's life if the situation improved.

The court rejected the submission of the Official Solicitor referred to above. Taylor LJ, at p 381B–E said this:

> 'The plight of Baby J is appalling and the problem facing the court in the exercise of its wardship jurisdiction is of the greatest difficulty. When should the court rule against the giving of treatment aimed at prolonging life?
> Three preliminary principles are not in dispute. First, it is settled law that the court's prime and paramount consideration must be the best interests of the child. That is easily said but not easily applied. What it does involve is that the views of the parents, although they should be heeded and weighed, cannot prevail over the court's view of the ward's best interests. In the present case the parents, finding themselves in a hideous dilemma have not taken a strong view so that no conflict arises.
> Secondly, the court's high respect for the sanctity of human life imposes a strong presumption in favour of taking all steps capable of preserving it, save in exceptional circumstances. The problem is to define those circumstances.
> Thirdly, and as a corollary to the second principle, it cannot be too strongly emphasised that the court never sanctions steps to terminate life. That would be unlawful. There is no question of approving, even in a case of the most horrendous disability, a course aimed at terminating life or accelerating death. The court is concerned only with the circumstances in which steps should not be taken to prolong life.'

This passage by Taylor LJ encompasses the three preliminary principles to be applied. Indeed, such approach has been endorsed in cases relating to incapacitated adults, including *Re R (Adult: Medical Treatment)* [1996] 2 FLR 99 at 107 and *Re H (A Patient)* [1998] 2 FLR 36 at 40.

The strong presumption in favour of prolonging life is not irrefutable. The court must balance all the evidence, giving due weight to the sanctity of life and looking at the problem, not from the point of view of the decider but from the assumed point of view of the patient. It is important to emphasise that even a very severely handicapped person may find a quality of life rewarding which to the unhandicapped might seem manifestly intolerable.

Taylor LJ, at p 383H put the matter in this way:

> 'I consider the correct approach is for the court to judge the quality of life the child would have to endure if given the treatment, and decide whether in all the circumstances such a life would be so afflicted as to be intolerable to that child. I say, 'to that child' because the test should not be whether the life would be tolerable to the decider. The test must be whether the child in question, if capable of exercising sound judgment, would consider the life tolerable. This is the approach adopted by McKenzie J in *Re Superintendent of Family and Child Service and Dawson* [1983] 145 DLR (3d) 610 in the passage at page 620 . . . .'

In the older case of *Re B (A Minor) (Wardship: Medical Treatment)* [1981] 1 WLR 1421, the balancing exercise led the Court of Appeal to override the refusal of parents to consent to an operation being carried out on their baby. The baby girl was born suffering from Down's syndrome and had an intestinal blockage from which she would die within a very short period of time unless she had an operation. If she had the operation, there was a considerable risk that she would suffer from heart trouble and die within two or three months. If, on the other hand, the operation was successful, she would have a life expectancy of some 20–30 years, during which time she would be very handicapped mentally and physically. The child was made a ward of court.

The local authority contended that the operation should go ahead, adding that provision would be made, if necessary, for the child to be cared for through long-term fostering or adoption. The parents opposed the operation, feeling that it was in their daughter's best interests to let nature take its course. The judge at first instance decided that it was in the child's best interests that she should not have the operation. The Court of Appeal disagreed and overruled the parents' refusal, stating that the operation should proceed.

Minors who are terminally ill
The test for the court in each and every case concerning a minor is the same. The court's prime and paramount consideration must be the best interests of the child.

In *Re C (A Minor) (Wardship: Medical Treatment)* [1990] Fam 26, a new-born baby suffering from congenital hydrocephalus was made a ward of court. The local authority sought the court's determination as to the appropriate manner in which she should be treated medically should she contract a serious infection, or her existing feeding regimes become unviable. Baby C was assessed as severely and irreversibly brain damaged. The prognosis was hopeless. The doctor, in whose charge the baby was, recommended that the objective of any treatment should therefore be to ease suffering rather than prolong her life. Whilst not specifying the adoption or discontinuance of any particular procedures, he further advised consultation with C's carers as to the appropriate method of achieving that objective. It was held that the court was entitled to approve, as being in her best interests, recommendations designed to ease her suffering rather than prolong life.

The 'no chance' situation
The 'no chance' situation is one of the five situations where the withholding or withdrawal of curative medical treatment might be considered, as set out in the Framework for Practice of the Royal College of Paediatrics and Child Health.

In *Re C (Medical Treatment)* [1998] 1 FLR 384, a child of 16 months was suffering from the fatal disease spinal muscular atrophy. Her doctors described her as being in a 'no chance' situation, meaning that her disease was so severe that life-sustaining treatment would simply delay death without significantly alleviating suffering and they considered such treatment inappropriate.

The child had been placed on ventilation to support her breathing. The doctor, in whose charge the child was, had come to the conclusion that it was not in the child's best interests for her to continue on indefinite ventilation, which would produce increasing distress and would inevitably involve a tracheotomy operation under anaesthetic, which might itself give rise to epilepsy, but that she should be taken off ventilation. He was further of the view that, if she were then, as was highly probable, to suffer a further respiratory relapse, it would be against her interests to seek to place her back on ventilation or indeed to engage in resuscitative treatment.

The hospital sought, through issuing an originating summons, the court's approval for the withdrawal of ventilation and non-resuscitation in the event of a respiratory arrest. The parents were prepared for ventilation to be withdrawn to see if their child would survive without it, but wished it to be reinstated in the event of further respiratory relapse.

The judge, Sir Stephen Brown, President of the Family Division, approached the course proposed by the hospital trust. The Framework for Practice was referred to the judge and particularly para 2.2.2 on p 10, where it was stated:

> '... withdrawal of treatment in paediatric intensive care units accounts for up to sixty five percent of deaths. Examples might be [and the second example is] the paediatric neurologist might reasonably withhold ventilator care in a child with progressive respiratory failure from anterior-horn cell disease.'

In this case the judge made an order in the following terms:

> 'There be leave to treat the minor C as advised by Doctor H, such treatment to include the withdrawal of artificial ventilation and non-resuscitation in the event of a respiratory arrest and palliative care to ease her suffering and permit her life to end peacefully and with dignity, such treatment being in C's best interest.'

A doctor cannot be required to treat a patient against his or her clinical judgment
No doctor can be required to treat a child, whether by the court, in the exercise of its wardship jurisdiction, by the parents, by the child or anyone else. The decision whether to treat is dependent upon an exercise of his or her own professional judgment, subject only to the threshold requirement that, save in exceptional circumstances of emergency, he or she has the consent of someone who has authority to give that consent (*Re R (A Minor) (Wardship: Medical Treatment)* [1992] 1 FLR 190 at 200).

This principle was drawn into sharp focus in *Re J (A Minor) (Medical Treatment)* [1992] 2 FLR 165. The child, aged 16 months, was severely handicapped, both mentally and physically, with a short expectation of life. He was placed with devoted foster carers by the local authority. His breathing had, on occasion, been assisted by the administration of oxygen. The doctor in whose charge the child was, was of the view that it would not be medically appropriate to intervene with intensive therapeutic measures, such as artificial ventilation, if the child were to suffer a life-threatening event.

The local authority applied to invoke the inherent jurisdiction of the High Court to determine whether artificial ventilation and/or other life-saving measures should be given to the child if he suffered a life-threatening event.

At a hearing on 12 May 1992, which was listed for the full hearing, but was treated as an interim hearing, the judge made an interim injunction, requiring the health authority, in the event of a life-threatening condition developing, to take all measures to prolong his life and provide artificial ventilation.

The Court of Appeal set aside the order, leaving the health authority free, subject to consent not being withdrawn, to treat J in accordance with their best clinical judgment. This left entirely to the doctors the decision whether or not to use mechanical ventilation in the light of changing circumstances. What the Court of Appeal firmly rejected was the suggestion that the medical practitioner in question should be required to treat the child in the way suggested and against his wishes or clinical recommendation. Lord Donaldson held that it would be an abuse of judicial power directly or indirectly to require the child to be treated contrary to the doctor's best clinical judgment.

In the case of *Re C (Medical Treatment)* [1998] 1 FLR 384, the court took the same approach, holding that the parents' contention that their child should be medically treated as they sought was tantamount to requiring the doctors to undertake a course of treatment which they were unwilling to do. It was held that the court could not consider making an order which would require the doctors to medically treat the child against their best clinical judgment.

Practice and procedure
Relief will be sought by originating summons in the Family Division. The court will be invited to exercise its parens patriae jurisdiction in relation to minors as part of the inherent jurisdiction of the High Court. When exercising such jurisdiction the court takes over the rights and duties of the parents. The parents' view and position will be of much importance but the responsibility for any decision will be that of the court alone.

Proceedings under the inherent jurisdiction are assigned to the Family Division and governed generally by the Rules of the Supreme Court and the Family Proceedings Rules. Part V of the FPR 1991 sets out the procedure to be followed when applying for wardship. An application to make a minor a ward of court is made by originating summons, together with an affidavit in support. Applications to the court in relation to minors should be made within wardship proceedings.

In relation to a next friend or guardian ad litem, r 9.2(1) of the FPR 1991 provides that, except as otherwise provided, a minor may begin and prosecute the proceedings only by his next friend and may defend the proceedings only by his guardian ad litem. Rule 9.2A of the FPR 1991 provides that, in certain circumstances, a minor may begin, prosecute or defend proceedings under the Children Act 1989 or the inherent jurisdiction of the High Court with respect to minors, without a next friend or guardian ad litem.

The applicants in an originating summons may be a health authority, or hospital trust, or a parent, or, indeed, a local authority, which has the child in its care, provided, in the latter case, that they have applied under s 100 of the Children Act 1989, for leave to invoke the inherent jurisdiction of the court and have been granted such leave. Where they are not an applicant, the parent or parents of the minor will be made defendants. A guardian ad litem – and it is usually the Official Solicitor – will be appointed to act for and on behalf of the minor.

There is no room for the application of the principles for the grant of interlocutory relief laid down in *American Cyanamid Company v Ethicon Limited* [1975] AC 396 in cases involving the medical treatment of minors (*Re J (A Minor) (Medical Treatment)* [1992] 2 FLR 165).

One exception to the basic rule that justice must be administered in public is where the court is exercising its jurisdiction in relation to minors. In cases of special difficulty and sensitivity in which the public interest requires that the court's decision and the reasons for it should be open to public scrutiny, the judge should give judgment in open court, setting out all the relevant facts and the medical and other considerations of which he or she has taken account, but taking all appropriate measures to preserve the personal privacy of those concerned (*Re C (A Minor) (Wardship: Medical Treatment)* [1990] Fam 26 at 37E).

Whilst drafting orders will materially differ from case to case, in the case of *Re C* [1990] Fam 26, where the doctors were not specifying the adoption or discontinuance of any particular procedure, but were recommending that the object of any treatment should be to ease suffering rather than prolong the life of the terminally ill child, it was held in the Court of Appeal to be inconsistent to give, within the terms of the order, specific instructions as to treatment. It was more appropriate in those circumstances for the court to approve the medical treatment as recommended by the doctors in whose charge the child was and the order of the court should be so drafted as to reflect that approval.

Chapter 6

ADULT REFUSAL OF MEDICAL TREATMENT: NON-CONSENSUAL TREATMENT

6.1 THE PRESUMPTION OF CAPACITY TO DECIDE

The thrust of this chapter is to consider the capacity or lack of capacity of an adult patient to consent to or refuse medical treatment.

Prima facie, every adult has the right and capacity to decide whether or not he or she will accept medical treatment, even if a refusal may risk permanent injury to his or her health or even lead to premature death. This is so, notwithstanding the very strong public interest in preserving the life and health of all citizens. This has been described as the conflict of principle between two interests. The first interest is that of the patient, and consists of his right to self-determination, even if it will damage his health or lead to premature death. The second interest is that of society in upholding the concept that all human life is sacred and that it should be preserved, if at all posssible. It is established that the right of the individual is paramount. Such a principle is evidenced, in stark terms, in two cases. First, *Home Secretary v Robb* [1995] 1 FLR 412 concerned a prisoner on hunger strike. He was of sound mind and understanding. It was held that the principle of self-determination required that effect be given to the patient's wishes; that a patient who refused treatment and in consequence died did not commit suicide nor did a doctor who complied with the patient's wishes aid and abet a suicide. In *St George's Healthcare NHS Trust v S; R v Collins and Others ex parte S* [1998] 2 FLR 728, a pregnant woman suffering from pre-eclampsia rejected the advice of a doctor that she needed urgent attention and admission to hospital for an induced delivery and that, without such treatment, her health and life and the life of the baby were in danger. She was admitted to a mental hospital against her will for assessment under s 2 of the Mental Health Act 1983. A judge was then requested to grant, and did grant, a declaration to the NHS trust dispensing with her consent to treatment and later that same evening her baby was born by Caesarean section. The Court of Appeal, in upholding her appeal against the declaration granted, held that, even though her own life and that of the baby were in danger, she was entitled to reject the advice offered and that the removal of the baby from within the body of the mother under physical compulsion amounted to trespass to the person.

6.2   ADULTS LACKING THE CAPACITY TO DECIDE

The presumption that every adult has the capacity to decide can be rebutted. A small number of the population lack the necessary mental capacity, due to mental illness or retarded development. This connotes a long-term or permanent lack of capacity to decide. There are, however, many adults who are ordinarily competent and of sound mind whose capacity may be diminished or extinguished by reason of temporary factors, such as pain, severe fatigue, drugs being used in their treatment, confusion or other effects of shock or unconsciousness.

If the patient does not have the required capacity to decide, the medical practitioner may treat the patient in what he or she believes to be in the patient's best interests.

6.3   ADJUDGING WHETHER OR NOT AN ADULT PATIENT HAS THE CAPACITY TO DECIDE

If the patient has the requisite capacity to decide, the doctor is bound by the patient's decision. If, on the other hand, the patient does not have the requisite capacity to decide, the doctor may treat the patient in what he or she believes to be the patient's best interests.

This distinction can present a particular dilemma for doctors, particularly in urgent and life-threatening circumstances. In cases of doubt as to the effect of a purported refusal of treatment, where failure to treat threatens the patient's life or threatens irreparable damage to his or her health, doctors and health authorities should not hesitate to apply to the courts for assistance (*Re T (An Adult) (Consent to Medical Treatment)* [1992] 2 FLR 458 at 474.

In the above case of *Re T*, the Court of Appeal set out the principles to be applied where an adult patient is refusing the treatment being medically advised according to the doctor's clinical judgment and the consequences of such refusal may have far-reaching consequences, including permanent injury or death ([1992] 2 FLR 458 at 473):

> '1. Prima facie every adult has the right and capacity to decide whether or not he will accept medical treatment, even if a refusal may risk permanent injury to his health or even lead to premature death. Furthermore, it matters not whether the reasons for the refusal were rational or irrational, unknown or even non-existent. This is so notwithstanding the very strong public interest in preserving the life and health of all citizens. However the presumption of capacity to decide, which stems from the fact that the patient is an adult, is rebuttable.
> 2. An adult patient may be deprived of his capacity to decide either by long-term medical incapacity or retarded development or by temporary factors such as unconsciousness or confusion or the effects of fatigue, shock, pain or drugs.
> 3. If an adult patient did not have the capacity to decide at the time of the purported refusal and still does not have that capacity, it is the duty of the doctors to treat him in

whatever way they consider, in the exercise of their clinical judgment, to be in his best interests.

4. Doctors faced with a refusal of consent have to give very careful and detailed consideration to what was the patient's capacity to decide at the time when the decision was made. It may not be a case of capacity or no capacity. It may be a case of reduced capacity. What matters is whether at that time the patient's capacity was reduced below the level needed in the case of a refusal of that importance, for refusals can vary in importance. Some may involve a risk to life or of irreparable damage to health. Others may not.

5. In some cases doctors will not only have to consider the capacity of the patient to refuse treatment, but also whether the refusal has been vitiated because it resulted not from the patient's will, but from the will of others. It matters not that those others sought, however strongly, to persuade the patient to refuse, so long as in the end the refusal represented the patient's independent decision. If, however, his will was overborne, the refusal will not have represented a true decision. In this context the relationship of the persuader to the patient – for example, spouse, parents or religious adviser – will be important, because some relationships more readily lend themselves to overbearing the patient's independent will than do others.

6. In all cases doctors will need to consider what is the true scope and basis of the refusal. Was it intended to apply in the circumstances which have arisen? Was it based upon assumptions which in the event have not been realised? A refusal is only effective within its true scope and is vitiated if it is based upon false assumptions.

7. Forms of refusal should be redesigned to bring the consequence of a refusal forcibly to the attention of patients.

8. In cases of doubt as to the effect of a purported refusal of treatment, where failure to treat threatens the patient's life or threatens irreparable damage to his health, doctors and health authorities should not hesitate to apply to the courts for assistance.'

At p 470 of *Re T*, Lord Donaldson confronted the difficult task of medical practitioners in adjudging capacity as follows:

'Doctors faced with a refusal of consent have to give very careful and detailed consideration to the patient's capacity to decide at the time when the decision was made. It may not be the simple case of the patient having no capacity because, for example, at that time he had hallucinations. It may be a more difficult case of a temporarily reduced capacity at the time when his decision was made. What matters is that the doctors should consider whether at that time he had a capacity which was commensurate with the gravity of the decision which he purported to make. The more serious the decision, the greater the capacity required. If the patient had the requisite capacity, they are bound by his decision. If not, they are free to treat him in what they believe to be his best interests.'

Assessment of Mental Capacity (published by the British Medical Association) is a report of the British Medical Association and The Law Society which incorporates guidance for doctors and lawyers on adjudging capacity. It provides practical guidance to both professions on circumstances where it may be necessary to assess a person's capacity, on how to assess capacity and highlighting any professional or ethical dilemmas that may arise.

6.3.1 *Re C* and the three-stage decision-making test as to capacity to decide

In *Re C (Refusal of Medical Treatment)* [1994] 1 FLR 31, the adult patient in question was unwilling to countenance the amputation of his leg, which was suffering from gangrene. He (the patient) sought from the hospital and was refused an undertaking that they would not amputate the leg in any future circumstances without his consent. The overall question was whether it had been established that the patient's capacity was so reduced by his chronic mental illness that he did not understand the nature, purpose and effects of the proposed treatment. Thorpe J, as he then was, accepted the medical evidence to the court that the decision-making process could be analysed in three stages. First, comprehending and retaining treatment information; secondly, believing it and, thirdly, weighing it in the balance to arrive at a choice. The judge determined that the patient had met, on the evidence, the three stage test and granted him the relief he sought by ruling that he was capable of refusing consent to medical treatment.

Proposals for reform

It is not unhelpful in this context to set out the proposed definition of 'persons without capacity' in the Draft Bill annexed to the Law Commission Report No 231 on Mental Incapacity.

Clause 2 of the draft is as follows:

'(1) for the purposes of this part of this Act a person is without capacity if at the material time—
(a) he is unable by reason of mental disability to make a decision for himself on the matter in question; or
(b) he is unable to communicate his decision on that matter because he is unconscious or for any other reason.
(2) for the purposes of this part of this Act a person is at the material time unable to make a decision by reason of mental disability if the disability is such that at the time when the decision needs to be made—
(a) he is unable to understand or retain the information relevant to the decision, including information about the reasonably foreseeable consequences of deciding one way or another or of failing to make the decision; or
(b) he is unable to make a decision based on that information, and in this Act "mental disability" means a disability or disorder of the mind or brain, whether permanent or temporary, which results in an impairment or disturbance of mental functioning.'

Clauses 1–5 of the Draft Bill referred to above are reproduced in Part III of this book.

6.3.2 Overriding a refusal of consent to treatment through lack of capacity

The patient's right of choice exists, whether the reasons for making that choice are rational, irrational, unknown or even non-existent. Nevertheless, an adult patient, in refusing consent to medical treatment, may lack capacity for the following reasons.

Non-competence

At the time of an apparent refusal of treatment, the patient may not, for the time being, be a competent adult. His or her understanding and reasoning powers may be seriously reduced by drugs or other circumstances, although he or she is not actually unconscious. It is vital to consider, in adjudging capacity or lack of capacity, whether the patient has a capacity commensurate with the gravity of the situation. In *Re MB (Medical Treatment)* [1997] 2 FLR 426, the patient fully consented and sought a Caesarean section operation. However, she could not bring herself to undergo the Caesarean section, since her fear of needles impeded the doctors in proceeding with the operation. On the evidence, it was determined by the court that the patient was temporarily incompetent. Her capacity was not commensurate with the gravity of the decision to be taken. A vaginal delivery would have posed a serious risk of death or brain damage to the baby. Her fear of needles and the panic it caused dominated her mind to the extent that she was incapable of making a decision at all.

Undue influence

A patient's refusal of consent may be invalid and vitiated through undue influence if it results, not from the patient's will, but from the will of others. The fundamental question is whether a refusal represents a patient's independent decision. There will not be undue influence simply because a patient is influenced and advised strenuously in his or her decision by others, provided that, in the end, the refusal represents his or her own independent decision. If, however, the will of the patient is overridden, the refusal will not have represented a true decision. The facts of each case need to be considered and the relationship between the patient and the adviser, whether a spouse, parents or religious adviser.

Re T (An Adult) (Consent for Medical Treatment) [1992] 2 FLR 458 concerned a patient whose mother was a Jehovah's Witness. The patient was 34 weeks pregnant and was involved in a car accident. While the patient's mother was with her, the patient had indicated to a staff nurse that she did not want a blood transfusion. The patient signed a pro forma refusal of consent to blood transfusions. When her condition deteriorated and she became unconscious, her father and another person applied to the court for a declaration that it would be lawful to administer a blood transfusion. The hospital had been abiding by the patient's refusal. It was held by the Court of Appeal that the patient's refusal was not a valid refusal and was not a genuine decision of the patient's, vitiated as it was by undue influence and varying other factors.

Changed circumstances

Another reason why an apparent refusal of consent may not be a true refusal is that it may not have been made with reference to the particular circumstances in which it turns out to be relevant. A patient who refuses consent in some circumstances does not necessarily give a true refusal of consent to treatment in any different circumstances which may arise. In all cases, doctors will need to consider the true scope and basis of the refusal – whether it was intended to apply in the circumstances which have arisen, whether it was based on assumptions which in the event have not been realised. A refusal can only be effective within its true scope and is vitiated if it is based upon false assumptions. In the case of *Re T*, the patient had refused consent to a blood transfusion in circumstances where she had been reassured that a blood transfusion was not often necessary, after a Caesarean section. Further, there was discussion with her as to alternative treatment available other than a blood transfusion. It was held that it could not be said that T understood the consequences of a continuing refusal to a blood transfusion in her changed deteriorating circumstances, given that there had been discussion earlier as to alternatives to a blood transfusion.

6.4   SPECIFIC CIRCUMSTANCES

6.4.1   Induced delivery: Caesarean section operation

The guidelines from the Royal College of Obstetricians and Gynaecologists entitled 'A Consideration of the Law and Ethics in relation to Court-Authorised Obstetric Intervention' give advice to members of the medical profession. The Committee concluded that:

> 'It is inappropriate and unlikely to be helpful or necessary to invoke judicial intervention to overrule an informed and competent woman's refusal of a proposed medical treatment, even though her refusal might place her life and that of her foetus at risk.'

The Court of Appeal has examined in much detail, in *Re MB (Medical Treatment)* [1997] 2 FLR 426 and *St George's Healthcare NHS Trust v S; R v Collins and Others ex parte S* [1998] 2 FLR 728, the circumstances in which it may or may not be lawful to carry out a Caesarian section operation on a patient if she is unwilling to consent to such an operation.

In *Re MB*, the patient had been willing to have a Caesarian section operation, as was advised to be medically necessary, but panicked at the last moment through her needle phobia when attempts were made to carry out the operation. She withdrew her consent to the operation. In circumstances where the patient was in labour and refused to agree to anaesthesia, the health authority applied for and was granted a declaration by the High Court judge that it would be lawful for the consultant gynaecologist to operate on her using reasonable force if necessary. The Court of Appeal dismissed the patient's appeal against the decision at first instance.

The Court of Appeal ruled that a competent adult patient has an absolute right to refuse to consent to medical treatment for any reason or for no reason at all, even where that decision might lead to his or her death. It is lawful, however, for doctors to be able to medically intervene in the absence of consent from the patient only where two circumstances pertain. First, the patient must lack competence. Secondly, the proposed treatment must be in the patient's best interests. On the particular facts of *Re MB*, the patient was, at the critical time, the court determined, suffering from an impairment of her mental functioning and was thereby temporarily incompetent.

The case of *St George's Healthcare NHS Trust v S* [1998] 2 FLR 728 sharply illustrates the presumption of capacity to decide and the principles of self-determination and autonomy of the patient; questions arose of unlawful admission to and detention in hospital. The patient, S, was 36 weeks pregnant. She had not sought ante-natal care. She was diagnosed as having pre-eclampsia, and advised that she needed urgent attention and admission to hospital for an induced delivery. Without this treatment, her health and life, and the health and life of her baby were in real danger. She fully understood the potential risks and rejected the advice. She was admitted to hospital against her will under the Mental Health Act 1983. An ex parte declaration was sought, and granted, by a judge, dispensing with her consent to treatment. Later that evening, she was delivered of a baby girl by Caesarean section. On appeal, the declaration by the judge at first instance was set aside. It was held that the patient was entitled not to be forced to submit to an invasion of her body against her will, notwithstanding the serious risks to her own life and that of her unborn child. Her right was not reduced or diminished, it was held, merely because her decision to exercise it might appear to be morally repugnant. The declaration of the judge at first instance involved the removal of the baby from within the body of the mother under physical compulsion. Unless lawfully justified, this amounted to an infringement of the mother's autonomy. Of themselves, the perceived needs of the foetus did not provide the necessary justification. The unlawful admission and detention of S under the Mental Health Act 1983 in this case is considered in Chapter 7 of this book.

In *Norfolk and Norwich Healthcare (NHS) Trust v W* [1996] 2 FLR 613, the patient arrived at hospital in labour. Throughout the day, she continued to deny she was pregnant. The obstetrician sought authority from the court to bring the patient's labour to an end by forceps delivery and, if necessary, a Caesarean section. It was held that, although the patient was not suffering from a mental disorder, she lacked the capacity and mental competence to make a decision about the proposed treatment because she was incapable of weighing up the considerations that were involved. Leave was granted to bring the labour to an end by forceps delivery and, if necessary, a Caesarean section.

In *Tameside and Glossop Acute Services Trust v CH* [1996] 1 FLR 762, the pregnant patient suffered from paranoid schizophrenia. She was resistant to treatment. Because of an intra-uterine growth retardation of the foetus, if the pregnancy was allowed to continue the foetus might have died in the womb. The trust applied to the court for authorisation to perform a Caesarean section, should it become necessary, if an induced labour was not successful, and to restrain the patient, if need be. The patient overwhelmingly lacked the capacity to consent to or refuse treatment. It was held that the proposed treatment, including the use of restraint, if clinically necessary, was within s 63 of the Mental Health Act 1983 and thus could be administered without her consent.

In the case of *Re S (Adult: Surgical Treatment)* [1993] 1 FLR 26, it was held that the Health Authority could lawfully perform an emergency Caesarean section operation on the patient on the grounds that it was in her and the unborn child's vital interests, despite the patient's refusal to give her consent and a declaration was granted to that effect.

In *Rochdale Healthcare (NHS) Trust v C* [1997] 1 FCR 274, the patient, who was in hospital for the birth of her child, would not agree to a Caesarean section as she had had a previous delivery in this way and subsequently suffered backache and pain around the resulting scar. She said she would rather die than have a Caesarean section again. The operation was required urgently and an application was made to the court less than an hour before it would need to be carried out. The consultant in charge was of the opinion that the patient seemed to be fully competent. It was held that an essential element in assessing a patient's capacity to decide whether or not to accept treatment was whether she was capable of weighing up the information she was given. In this case, the patient was in the throes of labour, with all that involved in terms of pain and emotional stress. The judge determined that a patient who, in those circumstances, could speak in terms which seemed to accept the inevitability of her own death, was not a patient who was able properly to weigh up the considerations that arose so as to make any valid decision. The court held that it would be in the best interests of the patient for the proposed procedure to be performed. Whilst the court was considering and determining the urgent application, it became apparent that the patient had in fact changed her mind and given her consent to the medical procedure. The operation, accordingly, was, in fact, performed with her consent and was successful for both the patient and the child.

The overall principles and effects flowing from the two major cases, *Re MB* and *St George's Healthcare NHS Trust v S*, already referred to, are as follows:

(a) A pregnant woman, who is an adult of sound mind, has an absolute right to refuse medical treatment, even if her own life and that of the unborn child depends on such treatment.

(b) Invasive surgery under physical compulsion cannot be justified on the basis of the needs of the foetus.

(c) A patient's right not to be forced to submit to an invasion of her body against her will is not reduced or diminished merely because her decision to exercise it may appear morally repugnant.

(d) The Mental Health Act 1983 cannot be used to detain a person against her will merely because her thinking process is unusual, even apparently bizarre and irrational, and contrary to the views of the overwhelming majority of the community at large. In *St George's Healthcare NHS Trust v S*, S was determined by the Court of Appeal to have been unlawfully admitted to, and detained in, hospital. This aspect of the case is further scrutinised in Chapter 7 of this book.

(e)   Even where lawfully detained under the Mental Health Act 1983, a patient is not deprived of all autonomy and cannot be forced into medical procedures, such as a Caesarian section operation unconnected with her mental condition, unless her capacity to consent to such treatment is diminished.

(f)   It is a criminal or tortious assault to perform physically invasive medical treatment without a patient's consent. In *St George's Healthcare NHS Trust v S*, the Caesarian section operation (together with the accompanying medical procedures) amounted to trespass on S. Whilst it might be available to defeat any claim based on aggravated or exemplary damages, the judge's decision at first instance, which was set aside by the Court of Appeal, would provide no defence to S's claim for damages for trespass against the relevant hospital.

(g)   It is lawful for doctors to intervene and carry out physically invasive treatment such as a Caesarian section operation without a patient's consent if the patient lacks the capacity to decide and is thus incompetent and the proposed medical treatment is in the best interests of the patient.

(h)   The Court of Appeal in *St George's Healthcare NHS Trust v S* set out guidelines to be followed in circumstances including where the possible need for Caesarian surgery is diagnosed and there is serious doubt about the patient's capacity to accept or decline treatment. These guidelines are appended in Part III of this book.

6.4.2   Fear of needles

In *Re MB (Medical Treatment)* [1997] 2 FLR 426, 40 weeks into the patient's pregnancy, it was found that the foetus was in the breach position. It was explained to the mother that a vaginal delivery would pose a serious risk of death or brain damage to the baby. She agreed to have a Caesarean section and was admitted to hospital and she and her partner agreed to the operation and signed a consent form.

In the case of *Re L (Patient: Non-Consensual Treatment)* [1997] 2 FLR 837, the patient was eight hours into her labour and her cervix had not dilated. The consultant obstetrician reached the view that, without intervention, the baby would die. The mother was keen to have her baby. She agreed in principle to a Caesarean section.

In each of the two cases above, however, the patients suffered a fear of needles which prevented the operations taking place. In each case, the health authority/trust applied for a declaration that it would be lawful to effect the treatment required by insertion of a needle for the purposes of anaesthesia and performance of an emergency Caesarean operation. The court held, in each instance, that the fear of needles and the panic involved impaired and disabled the patients' mental functioning. In each instance, the patient was held to be temporarily incompetent. Accordingly, in both cases the relief sought was acceded to by the court.

6.4.3   Blood transfusions

In *Re T (An Adult) (Consent to Medical Treatment)* [1992] 2 FLR 458, the patient was 34 weeks pregnant and suffered a road accident. Her mother was a practising Jehovah's Witness. While the mother was with her, the patient indicated that she did not want a blood transfusion. She signed a pro forma refusal of consent to such a blood transfusion. She was reassured that blood transfusions were often not necessary and that alternative options to a transfusion were available. The baby was stillborn. The patient's condition then deteriorated and she became unconscious. The consultant anaesthetist had wished to administer a blood transfusion but was inhibited from doing so by the patient's expressed wishes. The patient's father and friend applied to the court for a declaration that it was lawful for the hospital to administer a blood transfusion. The Court of Appeal held that the patient's refusal was not a valid and genuine decision, vitiated, as it was, by varying factors – the road accident, the ordeal and confusion she had been through and likely undue influence from her own mother. Nor could it be said that T understood the consequences of any continuing refusal in her changed deteriorating circumstances, given that there had been discussion earlier as to the alternatives to a blood transfusion. The declaration authorising a lawful blood transfusion was upheld.

6.4.4   Amputation

In *Re C (Refusal of Medical Treatment)* [1994] 1 FLR 31, surgeons at a hospital considered the patient would die imminently if his leg was not amputated below the knee. He had gangrene in his right foot. C refused to consider amputation. Alternative treatment was being tried and was successful but there was a likelihood of the gangrene recurring. C requested an undertaking from the hospital that it would not amputate the leg in any further circumstances. The hospital refused and C sought an injunction to restrain the hospital from amputating his right leg then or in the future without his expressed consent. It was held that, although his general capacity was impaired by schizophrenia, he had sufficiently understood the nature, purpose and effects of the treatment. He had understood and made a clear choice and, accordingly, relief would be granted in his favour.

6.4.5   Dialysis treatment

Re JT (Adult: Refusal of Medical Treatment) [1998] 1 FLR 48, concerned a woman of 25 suffering from mental disability. She developed renal failure. Eleven attempts were made to give her dialysis treatment. She resisted and then refused the treatment altogether. She made clear that she objected to dialysis and wanted to die. The judge carefully applied the three-stage test in *Re C*. It was clear that, notwithstanding her mental disability, she realised the consequences of refusal to continue treatment and that she had the capacity to decide to refuse the medical treatment in question.

In *Re D (Medical Treatment: Mentally Disabled Patient)* [1998] 2 FLR 22, the patient suffered from a long-standing psychiatric illness. He lacked the capacity to consent, or not consent, to treatment. He had developed a serious kidney complaint and required dialysis. He was, however, unable to co-operate with that treatment. The hospital authority sought the protection of the court in the form of a declaration that it was lawful not to impose treatment on D in the likely event that they continued to be unable to treat him. D was represented by the Official Solicitor. Declaratory relief was granted by the court in terms that, notwithstanding D's inability to consent to or refuse medical treatment, it would be lawful as being in his best interests for the hospital authority not to impose dialysis on him in circumstances in which it was not reasonably practicable so to do.

6.4.6 Hunger strikes

The general law is that an adult person of full mental capacity has the right to choose whether to eat or not. Even if the refusal to eat is tantamount to suicide, as in the case of a hunger strike, the adult in question cannot be compelled to eat or be forcibly fed. On the other hand, if a person lacks the mental capacity to choose, in common law the medical practitioner who has him in his care may treat him according to his clinical judgment of the patient's best interests (*B v Croydon Health Authority* [1995] 1 FLR 470).

Home Secretary v Robb [1995] 1 FLR 412, concerned a prisoner on hunger strike. He was 27 years old and had spent half his life in custody for criminal offences. It was agreed by all the medical and psychiatric experts assessing him that he was of sound mind and understanding. The patient's right of self-determination, it was held, was not diminished in the case of the defendant by his status as a detained prisoner. The principle of self-determination required that effect be given to his wishes and that a patient who refused treatment and, in consequence, died did not commit suicide, nor did a doctor who complied with the patient's wishes aid or abet a suicide. Declaratory relief was granted, as sought by the Home Secretary, that he could lawfully abide by the refusal of the defendant to receive nutrition and could lawfully abstain from providing hydration and nutrition whether by artificial means or otherwise for so long as the defendant retained the capacity to refuse the same.

6.5 THE USE OF REASONABLE FORCE AS A NECESSARY INCIDENCE OF TREATMENT

In *Norfolk and Norwich Healthcare (NHS) Trust v W* [1996] 2 FLR 613, the facts of which have been previously raised, it was held that the court did have power at common law in the circumstances arising to authorise the use of reasonable force as a necessary incidence of treatment.

In *Tameside and Glossop Acute Services Trust v CH* [1996] 1 FLR 762, the judge's view was that where, at common law, the question of the lawfulness of using restraint on a patient arose, an application should be made to the court seeking a determination that such treatment would be lawful.

In *Re MB (Medical Treatment)* [1997] 2 FLR 426, all that was involved, in this context, was the prick of a needle to enable the first part of anaesthesia to be given to the patient. In the event, no problem arose, since, following the court's determination, the patient finally co-operated and signed the consent form. However, in relation to the use of reasonable force, Butler-Sloss LJ at p 439 said as follows:

> 'In a number of first instance decisions the declarations have included that it would be lawful for reasonable force to be used in the course of such treatment. That declaration was granted . . . in the present case and is criticised . . . . It would however follow, in our view, from the decision that a patient is not competent to refuse treatment, that such treatment may have to be given against her continued objection if it is in her best interests that the treatment be given despite those objections. The extent of force or compulsion which may become necessary can only be judged in each individual case and by the health professionals. It may become for them a balance between continuing treatment which is forcibly opposed and deciding not to continue with it. This is a difficult issue which may have to be considered in greater depth on another occasion.'

6.6 PRACTICE AND PROCEDURE

The High Court, exercising its inherent jurisdiction, can rule by way of injunction or declaration that an individual is capable of refusing or consenting to medical treatment and can determine the effect of a purported advance direction as to future treatment. Such injunctive or declaratory relief can extend beyond the present to future circumstances (*Re C (Refusal of Medical Treatment)* [1994] 1 FLR 31).

In cases of real doubt as to the effect of a purported refusal of treatment, where failure to treat threatens the patient's life or threatens irreparable damage to his or her health, doctors and health authorities should not hesitate to apply to the court for assistance.

As is evidenced by the case of *Re JT (Adult: Refusal of Medical Treatment)* [1998] 1 FLR 48, where the medical experts had all been of the opinion that the patient had the requisite capacity and was competent to refuse treatment, there was no need to seek a declaration from the court to that effect.

In any cases involving serious doubt as to a patient's capacity, when surgical or invasive treatment may be needed, whether in relation to Caesarean surgery or otherwise, the Court of Appeal has laid down guidance as to procedure in both *Re T (An Adult) (Consent to Medical Treatment)* [1992] 2 FLR 458 and in *Re MB (Medical Treatment)* [1997] 2 FLR 426.

Such procedural advice and guidance has been developed and expanded in the case of *St George's Healthcare NHS Trust v S* [1998] 2 FLR 728. In that case, the Court of Appeal, after consultation with the President of the Family Division and the Official Solicitor at pp 758, 759 and 760 of the judgment set out detailed guidelines as to the practice and procedure to be followed in these type of cases. For example, the guidelines apply when the possible need for Caesarean surgery is diagnosed and there is serious doubt about the pregnant woman's capacity to accept or decline treatment. The guidelines further apply more generally to any other cases where surgical or invasive treatment may be needed by a patient whether male or female but there is real doubt as to the patient's capacity to accept or decline treatment.

These guidelines of the Court of Appeal are reproduced in Part III of this book. They will need to be carefully considered by all those involved in this field, including medical and health practitioners and hospital authorities, as well as legal practitioners. It is not intended here to repeat the purport of the guidelines. It is important to emphasise, however, under guideline [vii] that the hearing before the court should be inter partes. An order made in the patient's absence will not be binding on the patient unless he or she is represented either by a guardian ad litem (if incapable of giving instructions) or (if capable) by counsel or solicitor. Accordingly, a declaration granted ex parte without the patient being so represented will be of no assistance to the health authority or NHS trust. In the case of *St George's Healthcare NHS Trust v S*, the judge at first instance had erred in making a declaratory order on an ex parte application in proceedings which had not been instituted by the issue of the summons, without the patient's knowledge or even any attempt to inform her or her solicitor of the application, without any evidence, and without any provision to vary or discharge the order. This appeal against the grant of the declaration at first instance was allowed. It is important to emphasise and the guidelines themselves remind legal and medical practitioners that there may be occasions when there may be a serious question about the competence of a patient and the situation facing the authority may be so urgent and the consequences so desperate that it will be impracticable to attempt to comply with the guidelines. As it is put in the conclusion to the guidelines, 'where delay may itself cause serious damage to the patient's health or put her life at risk then formulaic compliance with these guidelines would be inappropriate'.

Chapter 7

MEDICAL TREATMENT AND THE MENTALLY ILL

7.1 SELF-DETERMINATION AND THE MENTALLY ILL

In relation to those suffering from mental illness, as with those who are not, consent is required from a patient before medical treatment can be given.

It is emphasised by the Law Commission in its report on Mental Incapacity (No 231) that, wherever possible, and particularly in relation to the vulnerable, who are or may be mentally ill, the principle of self-determination and autonomy of the individual must apply and be further encouraged.

The Mental Health Act 1983 Code of Practice, issued by the Department of Health and Welsh Office, stresses the necessity of providing patients with sufficient information to enable them to understand the nature, purpose and likely effect of the treatment and to inform the patient of any viable alternatives. The Code goes further and says the patient should be advised of his or her right to withdraw consent at any time during the period of treatment.

7.1.1 The test as to capacity to consent

In *Re C (Refusal of Medical Treatment)* [1994] 1 FLR 31, an adult patient who was suffering from gangrene in one of his legs was advised by doctors that there was a large chance of imminent death if the leg was not amputated. The adult patient was unwilling to countenance the amputation of the leg and sought assurances from the hospital that his wishes would be respected then and in the future. In determining whether an adult patient does or does not have the capacity to decide, the judge applied a three-stage test:

(1) whether the adult patient could comprehend and retain the treatment information;
(2) whether the adult patient believed it;
(3) whether the adult patient could weigh it in the balance to arrive at a choice.

The adult patient in that case was determined by the court to pass the three-stage test and, accordingly, it was held that he was able to understand the nature, purpose and effects of the proposed treatment. The three-stage test in *Re C* has been, and continues to be, a yardstick by which, at common law, to measure whether or not an adult patient lacks capacity.

The Law Commission appended to its report on Mental Incapacity (No 231) the draft of a Bill in relation to mentally incapacitated persons. This Draft Bill has not passed into legislation. Nevertheless, it is not unhelpful, in the context of the mentally ill, to recite a part of cl 2 of the Draft Bill dealing with 'persons without capacity'.

Clause 2(2) of the Draft Bill is as follows:

> 'For the purposes of this part of this Act a person is at the material time unable to make a decision by reason of mental disability if the disability is such that at the time when the decision needs to be made—
> (a) he is unable to understand or retain the information relevant to the decision, including information about the reasonably foreseeable consequences of deciding one way or another or of failing to make the decision; or
> (b) he is unable to make a decision based on that information, and in this Act 'mental disability' means a disability or disorder of the mind or brain, whether permanent or temporary, which results in an impairment or disturbance of mental functioning.'

7.1.2 A person suffering from mental disorder is not necessarily incapable of giving or refusing consent to treatment

The fact that a person is suffering from mental illness does not automatically mean that he or she lacks the capacity to decide. To ascertain the common law position in this regard, it is helpful to scrutinise briefly four cases in each of which it was held that doctors were bound by the decision of the patient to refuse treatment, notwithstanding any mental health problems they had.

In *Re C* [1994] 1 FLR 31, which has been referred to previously at **7.1.1**, the adult patient in question had been diagnosed as suffering from chronic paranoid schizophrenia and had been transferred to Broadmoor, where he was treated with drugs and ECT. This had resulted in some improvement and he was on an open ward. Notwithstanding his mental health difficulties and background, it was held that he had the capacity to refuse the medical treatment advised. The patient was quite content to follow medical advice and co-operate with treatment as long as his rejection of amputation was respected.

In *Re JT (Adult: Refusal of Medical Treatment)* [1998] 1 FLR 48, the court was concerned with a patient, a woman of 25, who suffered from mental disability involving learning difficulties and extremely severe behavioural disturbance. She was found to have developed renal failure. Eleven attempts were made to give her dialysis treatment, most of them resisted by the patient, and, thereafter, she refused any further treatment. There was no feasible alternative treatment. The patient consistently told the doctor and both psychiatrists concerned with the case and members of her family that she objected to dialysis and wanted to die. It was held to be clear on the evidence that the patient understood the information given to her as to the purpose of dialysis treatment and its nature, that she believed it, that she realised the consequences of refusal to continue treatment, and that she had the capacity to make a decision about giving or refusing agreement to treatment in accordance with the three-stage test laid down in *Re C*. Declarations were granted by the court that the patient was capable of refusing medical treatment and also that it was lawful for the hospitals in question to abide by her refusal and not perform renal dialysis on her.

The case of *Home Secretary v Robb* [1995] 1 FLR 412 concerned a prisoner on hunger strike. He was then aged 27 and had spent at least half his life in custody for criminal offences and suffered from a personality disorder evidenced by a number of factors including addiction to drugs and violent tendencies. It was agreed, however, by all the medical and psychiatric experts assessing him that he was of sound mind and understanding. Relief was granted by the court to the effect that the Home Secretary might lawfully observe and abide by the refusal of the prisoner to receive nutrition, and further that the Home Secretary might lawfully abstain from providing hydration and nutrition, whether by artificial means or otherwise, for so long as the prisoner retained the capacity to refuse food or drink. The court emphasised again the principle of self-determination which required that effect be given to a patient's wishes providing that he or she has the capacity to make a choice. It was further held that a patient who refuses treatment and in consequence dies does not commit suicide nor does a doctor who complies with the patient's wishes aide or abet a suicide.

In *St George's Healthcare NHS Trust v S; R v Collins and Others ex parte S* [1998] 2 FLR 728 a woman who was 36 weeks pregnant was admitted to hospital under the Mental Health Act 1983 against her will in circumstances where she was suffering from pre-eclampsia and refusing voluntarily to be admitted to hospital for an induced delivery or Caesarean section. She had been advised that without hospital treatment her health and life, and the life of her baby, were in danger. Notwithstanding such advice, and fully understanding the potential risks, the patient rejected such advice since she wanted her baby to be born naturally. It was held in the Court of Appeal that the fact that she was jeopardising her own life and that of the baby did not connote any form of mental illness. Even though her choice might appear to most either morally repugnant or irrational, she was fully entitled, the Court of Appeal held, not to be treated in hospital against her wishes, even if she was thereby risking her own life and that of the unborn child. She was determined by the court to have the capacity to make a choice.

The Code of Practice under the Mental Health Act 1983 states at 15.11:

> 'A person suffering from a mental disorder is not necessarily incapable of giving consent. Capacity to consent is variable in people with mental disorder and should be assessed in relation to the particular patient, at the particular time, as regards the particular treatment proposed. Not every one is equally capable of understanding the same explanation of a treatment plan. A person is more likely to be able to give valid consent if the explanation is appropriate to the level of his assessed ability.'

At common law, a person who ordinarily has the capacity to consent or refuse to consent to treatment, notwithstanding that he or she may suffer from mental illness, may be given medical treatment in the absence of his or her consent in the circumstances of an emergency.

7.1.3 Caesarian section operations and the Mental Health Act 1983

The basic facts of the *St George's Healthcare NHS Trust v S* case have been set out above. S was rejecting medical treatment which was advised to be urgently necessary for her own health and that of the unborn child.

S was admitted to hospital – the Springfield Psychiatric Hospital – under s 2 of the Mental Health Act 1983.

Section 2(2) of the Act is as follows:

> 'An application for admission for assessment may be made in respect of a patient on the grounds that –
>
> (a) he is suffering from mental disorder of a nature or degree which warrants the detention of the patient in a hospital for assessment (or for assessment followed by medical treatment) for at least a limited period; and
> (b) he ought to be so detained in the interests of his own health and safety or with a view to the protection of other persons.'

The Court of Appeal determined that the application for admission under s 2 was unlawful and appropriate declaratory relief was granted by the court in S's favour. While satisfied that the requirements of s 2(2)(b) might well have been fulfilled, the cumulative grounds prescribed in s 2(2)(a), the Court of Appeal held, were not established. Those involved in the decision to make an application for admission under s 2 had failed to maintain the distinction between the urgent need of S for treatment arising from her pregnancy and the separate question whether her mental disorder (in the form of depression) warranted her detention in hospital. There was no evidence that S had been detained in order to assess or treat any such mental disorder. Rather, she had been detained in order that adequate provision could be made to deal with S's pregnancy and the safety of her unborn child.

It was further held that S's transfer to, and the period while she was detained at, St George's Hospital, where the child was born, were both unlawful. S was, therefore, wrongly detained throughout the period when she was in St George's Hospital and throughout the operative procedures which were carried out on her, in accordance with the declaration granted by the judge at first instance.

Important principles emanate from *St George's Healthcare NHS Trust v S* in relation to the use, or possible use, of the provisions of the Mental Health Act 1983 where invasive surgery such as that of a Caesarian section operation may be necessary.

First, the Mental Health Act 1983 cannot be deployed to achieve the detention of an individual against her will merely because her thinking process is unusual, even apparently bizarre and irrational, and contrary to the views of the overwhelming majority of the community at large.

Secondly, even where a person is lawfully detained under the Mental Health Act 1983, she is not deprived of all autonomy and cannot be forced into medical procedures such as a Caesarian section operation unconnected with her mental condition unless her capacity to consent to such treatment is diminished. This aspect is further examined when considering s 63 of the Mental Health Act 1983 later in this chapter.

7.2 PATIENTS LACKING THE CAPACITY TO GIVE OR REFUSE CONSENT TO MEDICAL TREATMENT

In relation to a patient who fails the test as to capacity, and in the absence of consent, a doctor may only treat such a patient as is permitted by the common law or statute.

In the case of *Re F (Mental Patient: Sterilisation)* [1990] 2 AC 1, it was held that treatment of a patient in common law is lawful if it is in his or her best interests. Such treatment would be in his or her best interests, as Lord Brandon said at p 55:

'If it is carried out to save lives or ensure improvement or prevent deterioration in their physical or mental health.'

The standard by which to measure whether or not a doctor is acting in the best interests of the incapacitated patient is the test laid down in *Bolam v Friern Hospital Management Committee* [1957] 1 WLR 582, namely that he or she must act in accordance with a practice accepted at the time by a responsible body of medical opinion skilled in the particular form of treatment in question. In the case of *Re F*, the House of Lords rejected the view of the Court of Appeal in the case that a more stringent test was required than the *Bolam* test for adults lacking capacity. A more stringent test for those adults who are incompetent, the House of Lords held, could result in such adults being deprived, in some circumstances, of the benefit of medical treatment which adults who are competent to give consent, enjoy.

The case of *Re F* further decided that, in the absence of parens patriae jurisdiction for adults, any jurisdiction to approve or disapprove of medical treatment for and on behalf of an incapacitated adult does not exist. No one, including the court, accordingly can give consent or refuse consent to treatment for those mentally ill adults who lack capacity.

In the case of *In Re F* at p 69, Lord Griffiths summarised the position as follows:

'In a civilised society the mentally incompetent must be provided with medical and nursing care and those who look after them must do their best for them. Stated in legal terms the doctor who undertakes responsibility for the treatment of the mental patient who is incapable of giving consent to treatment must give the treatment that he considers to be in the best interests of his patient and the standard of care required of the doctor will be that laid down in *Bolam* ...'.

The court in its inherent jurisdiction is able, however, to declare that proposed medical treatment is lawful as being in a patient's best interests, or not lawful as not being in the patient's best interests.

The jurisdiction for a doctor to be able to treat, without his or her consent, an adult who lacks capacity lies in the common law principle of necessity (*Re F* [1990] 2 AC 1 and *R v Bournewood Community and Mental Health NHS Trust ex parte L* [1998] 2 FLR 550).

7.2.1   The Enduring Power of Attorney Act 1985

This Act allows a person whilst competent to appoint a person of his or her choice (agent or attorney) who is legally empowered to act for him or her if he or she becomes mentally incapable. Such agent or attorney then has various powers, but is not entitled to decide on questions of healthcare and medical treatment for and on behalf of the patient.

7.3   INFORMALITY OF DECISION-TAKING IN RELATION TO THOSE ADULTS LACKING CAPACITY

Regular decisions are taken by medical practitioners or other health carers, day-to-day, for and on behalf of those adults lacking capacity, without any recourse to the courts. Many patients suffering from mental illness who lack capacity do so for a long period or permanently. Many of the medical decisions taken are mundane, some less than mundane. Issues of capacity to decide from the patient's point of view may never arise or be tested and there must be a grey area as to the legal basis on which some of these decisions are made and as to whether, on occasions and unwittingly, doctors or other health carers may be exceeding their authority to treat the patient.

The Mental Health Act 1983 Code of Practice states at 15.20:

> 'The administration of medical treatment to people incapable of taking their own treatment decisions is a matter of much concern to professionals and others involved in their care. It is the personal responsibility of professionals to ensure that they understand the relevant law.'

In this context, cl 4 of the Draft Bill of the Law Commission, appended to its report on Mental Incapacity (No 231) contains at subcl 1 the following wording:

> '... It shall be lawful to do anything for the personal welfare or health care of a person who is, or is reasonably believed to be, without capacity in relation to the matter in question ... if it is in all the circumstances reasonable for it to be done by the person who does it.'

7.4   INFORMAL ADMISSIONS TO HOSPITAL UNDER THE MENTAL HEALTH ACT 1983

Patients may be admitted to hospital under the Mental Health Act 1983, either informally or formally. The informal admission of patients is under s 131 of the Act. What fell for decision in the case of *R v Bournewood Community and Mental Health NHS Trust ex parte L* [1998] 2 FLR 550, was what category or categories of patients come within s 131 as being suitable for informal admission.

The Court of Appeal had held that those who, though lacking capacity to consent, do not object to admission to hospital ('compliant incapacitated patients') do not fall within s 131 and are not within the category of an informal patient.

The House of Lords, in allowing the appeal from the Court of Appeal and having more background to the intention which lay behind the passing into legislation of the statutory provision in question, held that s 131 of the Act should be so construed that such patients described above, namely those who are 'compliant incapacitated patients', do fall within s 131 and can be admitted as informal patients to hospital.

The Percy Commission and its consequent report had pointed the way in suggesting that there would be less stigma for patients and their families, and thus more incentive and encouragement for them to receive medical help, if patients could be readily admitted to hospital without a formal admission and the consequences flowing from that. The Court of Appeal, however, had pointed out that one of the consequences – and a significant one – for those patients admitted informally was that they were not able to avail themselves of all the statutory safeguards in the Mental Health Act 1983 available to those formally admitted.

The case of *L* has clarified the legal basis, in the absence of any statutory provision, for the medical treatment of those adult patients informally admitted to hospital. The justification for such medical treatment lies in the common law principle of necessity.

Lord Steyn at the end of his judgment in the case of *L* at p 569 said this:

> 'The common law principle of necessity is a useful concept, but it contains none of the safeguards of the Act of 1983. It places effective and unqualified control in the hands of the hospital psychiatrist and other healthcare professionals. It is, of course, true that such professionals owe a duty of care to patients and that they will almost invariably act in what they consider to be the best interests of the patient. But neither habeas corpus nor judicial review are sufficient safeguards against misjudgements and professional lapses in the case of compliant incapacitated patients. Given that such patients are diagnostically indistinguishable from compulsory patients, there is no reason to withhold the specific and affective protection of the Act of 1983 from a large class of vulnerable mentally incapacitated individuals. Their moral right to be treated with dignity requires nothing less. The only comfort is that Counsel for the Secretary of State have assured the House that reform of the law is under active consideration.'

7.5 THE MENTAL HEALTH ACT 1983

The common law applies to patients detained under the Mental Health Act 1983, save and insofar as specific statutory provision is made under the Act, and particularly under Part IV of the Act.

The detained status of patients, of itself, does not imply inability to give consent. As predicated at 16.4 of the Code of Practice:

'For all treatments proposed for a detained patient and which may be lawfully given under the Act it is necessary first to seek the patient's agreement and consent.'

7.5.1 The meaning of medical treatment

Section 145 of the Mental Health Act 1983 defines medical treatment for the purposes of the Act. Such medical treatment includes, 'nursing and care, habilitation and rehabilitation under medical supervision', namely the broad range of activities aimed at alleviating or preventing a deterioration of the patients' mental disorder. It includes physical treatment such as electro-consulsive therapy (ECT) and the administration of drugs and psychotherapy.

7.5.2 Part IV

Part IV applies only to medical treatment for mental disorder. It provides specific statutory authority for forms of medical treatment for mental disorder to be given to most detained patients without their consent in certain circumstances and with certain safeguards.

Section 57
This section pertains to medical treatment of the most serious kind with ethical and public policy concerns, namely psychosurgery (such as surgery in relation to brain tissue) and the surgical implantation of hormones for the reduction of male sexual drive.

The safeguards of the requirement of both expressed consent by the patient and a second opinion apply to informally admitted patients as well as to those detained. As Lord Griffiths at p 69 of *Re F* [1990] 2 AC 1 pointed out, these types of treatments can never be carried out, however necessary, in the absence of consent by the patient. Such treatment accordingly can never be implemented on an adult lacking capacity to consent, whether under the guise of any common law principle of necessity or otherwise.

Section 58
Treatment by ECT at any time, and the administration of medicine beyond three months, may only be effected if the patient has provided a valid consent (and this will always be sought of the patient) or a second opinion is obtained.

These safeguards apply to all patients liable to be detained except those detained under s 4, s 5(2) or (4), s 35, s 135, s 136 and s 37(4); also patients conditionally discharged under s 42(2) and ss 73 and 74. All these patients can only be treated under common law.

Section 63

Apart from the treatments specifically mentioned in ss 57 and 58, other forms of medical treatment for the mental disorder from which the patient is suffering may be given without the patient's consent being obtained.

Section 63 covers a wide range of therapeutic activities involving a variety of professional staff and includes, in particular, psychological and social therapies.

In practice, medical staff will seek the consent of the patient and it is unlikely that most of these activities could be undertaken without the patient's acceptance and active co-operation.

In the case of *Tameside and Glossop Acute Services Trust v CH* [1996] 1 FLR 762, the defendant patient was aged 41 at the time and had suffered from paranoid schizophrenia since 1983. In 1995, she was admitted to the psychiatric wing of the hospital under s 3 of the Act and it was discovered that she was pregnant. She wished to have the baby but was apt to resist treatment. She clearly lacked capacity. An intra-uterine growth retardation of the foetus was discovered and the medical view taken was that if the pregnancy was allowed to continue the foetus might die in the womb. The doctors wished to induce labour and, given that the patient lacked capacity and might actively resist, the trust applied to the court for authorisation to perform a Caesarean section should it become necessary, restraining the patient if need be. The court held that the proposed treatment, including the use of restraint if clinically necessary, was treatment given for the mental disorder from which she was suffering within s 63 of the Act. Accordingly, by virtue of that section, the treatment could be administered without her consent. The reasons for the proposed treatment falling within s 63 were as follows. First, an ancillary reason for the induction and, if necessary, the Caesarean section, was to prevent a deterioration of the patient's mental state. Secondly, for the treatment of her schizophrenia to be effective, it was necessary for her to give birth to a live baby. Thirdly, her treatment required her to receive strong anti-psychotic medication which had been interrupted by pregnancy and could not be resumed until the child was born.

Whether and to what extent the reasoning in the *Tameside* case in relation to s 63 is still applicable must be cast into doubt by the case of *St George's Healthcare NHS Trust v S; R v Collins and Others ex parte S* [1998] 2 FLR 728. There, the Court of Appeal reasoned that s 63 may apply to the treatment of any condition which is 'integral' to the mental disorder of the patient. The question is whether a Caesarian section can be viewed as treatment for a patient's mental disorder. The view of the Court of Appeal was that, in the final analysis, a woman detained under the Act for mental disorder cannot be forced into medical procedures unconnected with her mental condition unless her capacity to consent to such treatment is diminished. It would appear, accordingly, to be the case that, where a woman patient is detained under the Act and the question arises as to whether an induced delivery and/or Caesarian section should be carried out, the essential consideration will be her capacity to decide. When she retains her capacity, her consent will remain an essential prerequisite and whether she does or does not have the capacity to decide will have to be determined on the basis of the circumstances in each individual case.

In *B v Croydon Health Authority* [1995] 1 FLR 470, the patient, a woman of 24 was detained in hospital under s 3 of the Act suffering from a psychopathic disorder with symptoms including a compulsion to self-harm. She virtually stopped eating and was threatened with feeding by naso-gastric tube. An application was made on her behalf for an injunction restraining the health authority from feeding the patient by tube without her consent. It was held that she could be lawfully fed in such a manner without her consent under s 63 of the Act. Given the wide definition of s 145(1) namely that 'treatment' included nursing and care concurrent with the core treatment or as a necessary prerequisite to such treatment, it was held by the court that it must follow that the term 'medical treatment ... for the mental disorder' in s 63 included treatment given to alleviate the symptoms of the disorder as well as treatment to remedy its underlying cause.

Section 62
In certain circumstances, the provisions of ss 57 and 58 of the Act do not apply where urgent treatment is required. Section 62 is not applicable to any forms of treatment other than those set out in ss 57 and 58.

The Code of Practice, at 16.18, gives guidance, to the effect that it is insufficient for the proposed treatment to be simply necessary or beneficial. It must be immediately necessary to achieve one of the objects set out in s 62. It is further advised that 'in certain circumstances hazardous or irreversible treatment cannot be administered under this section, even if it is immediately necessary.'

7.6   PROPOSAL FOR REFORM OF THE LAW RELATING TO MENTAL INCAPACITY

There is presently consultation on reform of the law relating to decision-making on behalf of mentally incapacitated adults. This process has been commenced through the consultation paper issued by the Lord Chancellor's department in December of 1997 and entitled 'Who decides? Making Decisions on behalf of Mentally Incapacitated Adults'.

The Law Commission Report on Mental Incapacity (No 231) and the Government's Green Paper, 'Who decides?' suggest a single piece of legislation to make a new provision for those who lack mental capacity. Statutory definitions of the 'best interests test' and of lack of capacity are proposed, as well as statutory protection for those making, day-to-day, a wide range of informal decisions, small or large, for those adults who are incapacitated. Statutory provision, importantly, is suggested to allow the court and others to make decisions for and on behalf of those adults lacking capacity. There is discussion of, and proposals as to, accordingly, delegated consents and continuing powers of attorney, as well as a statutory basis for advance refusals of medical treatment. A suggestion is that the new statutory jurisdiction would be operated by the courts with an extension to the jurisdiction of the Court of Protection assisted administratively by the Public Trust office. One option advocated is the establishment of a new superior court of record called the Court of Protection, in place of the current Court of Protection. The jurisdiction currently operated by the Court of Protection is very small, but the Law Commission suggested its jurisdiction might be exercised by a judge or judges nominated by the Lord Chancellor. However, it must be emphasised that, as yet, the recommendations of the Law Commission have not been implemented by Parliament.

Chapter 8

MINORS: CONSENT OR REFUSAL OF CONSENT TO MEDICAL TREATMENT

8.1 DEFINITION OF A MINOR

A minor is a person who has not attained the age of 18 years (s 1(1) of the Family Law Reform Act 1969). The corresponding definition of a child is set out in s 105 of the Children Act 1989. The use of the wording 'an immature minor' below refers to a minor who is not '*Gillick*-competent'. That a minor is 'immature' will ordinarily be obvious by reason of his or her age. The relevant test as to competency in respect of the older minor is considered at **8.4.1**.

8.2 PARENTAL CONSENT TO MEDICAL TREATMENT FOR AND ON BEHALF OF THE IMMATURE MINOR

8.2.1 The general requirement of consent before treatment

'It is trite law that, in general, a doctor is not entitled to treat a patient without the consent of someone who is authorised to give that consent. If he does so, he will be liable in damages for trespass to the person and may be guilty of a criminal assault . . .'

(*Re R (A Minor) (Wardship: Medical Treatment)* [1992] 1 FLR 190 at 196).

8.2.2 Emergencies

In an emergency or exceptional circumstances (such as abandonment of the child or inability to find the parent), a doctor may treat a child without parental knowledge and consent.

8.2.3 Parental responsibility

A parent or parents or other person or body with parental responsibility will ordinarily consent to treatment for and on behalf of the minor, unless and until such minor himself or herself has the capacity to consent.

'Parental responsibility' means 'all the rights, duties, powers, responsibilities and authority which by law a parent of a child has in relation to the child and his property' (s 3 of the Children Act 1989). That section of the Act includes the right of a person with parental responsibility to consent to medical treatment for and on behalf of a child. Valid consent to medical treatment of the immature minor is, accordingly, obtained from a person who has parental responsibility for that minor. The position of the mother and father of a child in relation to parental responsibility may be seen in ss 2 and 4 of the 1989 Act. Other persons who obtain a residence order in respect of a child will have parental responsibility for that child. A local authority which has a care order in relation to a child will have parental responsibility for such child pursuant to s 33(3)(a) of the Children Act 1989.

Section 2(9) of the Act permits a person with parental responsibility 'to arrange for some or all of it to be met by one or more persons acting on his behalf'. This statutory provision does not permit a person with parental responsibility to surrender or transfer any part of his or her parental responsibility but might envisage, for example, a mother who is abroad for a period to delegate her authority to consent to medical treatment for the child to a relative. To what extent a consent to treatment by such a person would be treated by a medical practitioner as valid is untested and might depend, for example, on the scope of the arrangement between the mother and relative, the proof in writing or otherwise of such arrangement and the type of treatment required. Again, in relation to s 3(5) of the Children Act 1989, it is untested as to what extent, if at all, a person who does not have parental responsibility for a child but has de facto care may consent to any medical treatment for and on behalf of the child or have any such consent accepted as valid.

It would certainly appear to be reasonable within s 3(5) for someone caring for a child, where the parent or parents are absent, to arrange routine medical treatment. In circumstances where the child may require more significant medical treatment, however, questions would inevitably arise as to whether the parents' permission could be sought and obtained. The consequences to the child of delaying any medical treatment would also, no doubt, be a factor for consideration. If the health of a child were seriously at risk and whether or not the terms of s 3(5) applied, the common law principles of necessity would entitle medical practitioners in the absence of parental consent to effect treatment which was in the best interests of the child. The agreement of the de facto carers to the medical treatment advised to be taken by the doctors in those circumstances would undoubtedly assist the child and doctors to reduce the scope for any controversy upon the re-appearance of the parent or parents with parental responsibility.

8.2.4 Disagreement between parents

A mother of a child – whether or not she and the father were married at the date of birth of the child – will have parental responsibility for that child. The father of a child will have parental responsibility for that child if, at the date of birth, he and the mother were married (s 2 of the Children Act 1989). If they were not so married, the father may acquire parental responsibility either by the mother and father entering into a 'parental responsibility agreement', as designated under the appropriate regulations or by the father applying to the court for an order granting him parental responsibility under s 4 of the Act. If the father has parental responsibility, he and the mother of the child may disagree as to proposed medical treatment for their child. As a matter of law, the consent of either parent will authorise such medical treatment. As was said in *Re R (A Minor) (Wardship: Medical Treatment)* [1992] 1 FLR 190 at 196:

> 'If the parents disagree, one consenting and the other refusing, the doctor will be presented with a professional and ethical but not with a legal problem because, if he has the consent of one authorised person, the treatment will not without more constitute a trespass or a criminal assault.'

8.3 PARENTAL REFUSAL OF MEDICAL TREATMENT FOR AND ON BEHALF OF THE IMMATURE MINOR: OVERRIDING SUCH REFUSAL

A parent or parents or other person or body with parental responsibility will ordinarily be entitled to refuse treatment for and on behalf of the minor, unless and until such minor achieves the necessary capacity himself or herself under the test in *Gillick v West Norfolk and Wisbech Area Health Authority* [1986] AC 112.

The court has the power under its parens patriae jurisdiction to overrule, if required, the refusal of a parent or parents to consent to medical treatment for and on behalf of an immature child.

8.3.1 The test for the court

The court's prime and paramount consideration will be the best interests of the minor (*Re J (A Minor) (Wardship: Medical Treatment)* [1991] 1 FLR 366 at 381. The court will scrutinise and balance the evidence presented to reach a decision in the best interests of the child.

8.3.2 The views of the parents and the court's balancing exercise

Since it is the parents' view which may or may not be overruled by the court, necessarily their views and the reasons for their refusal of proposed medical treatment for their child must be carefully considered. Per Sir Thomas Bingham MR in *Re Z (A Minor) (Identification: Restrictions on Publication)* [1997] Fam 1 at 32–33:

> 'I would for my part accept without reservation that the decision of a devoted and responsible parent should be treated with respect. It should certainly not be disregarded or lightly set aside. But the role of the Court is to exercise an independent and objective judgment. If that judgment is in accord with that of the devoted and responsible parent, well and good. If it is not, then it is the duty of the Court, after giving due weight to the view of the devoted and responsible parent, to give effect to its own judgment. That is what it is there for. Its judgment may of course be wrong. So may that of the parent. But once the jurisdiction of the Court is invoked its clear duty is to reach and express the best judgment it can.'

Liver transplant operation

In *Re T (A Minor) (Wardship: Medical Treatment)* [1997] 1 FLR 502, T was born in April of 1995 with a life-threatening liver defect and an operation when he was three and a half weeks old was unsuccessful. The unanimous medical prognosis was that he would not live beyond the age of two to two and a half years without a liver transplant. It was equally the unanimous clinical opinion of the consultants that it was in his best interests to undergo the operation when a donor liver became available. The parents, healthcare professionals, had gone with their baby son to live and work abroad. They did not wish him to undergo a transplant and refused consent to an operation should a suitable liver become available. The doctors in England treating T referred the matter to the relevant local authority, which applied, pursuant to s 100(3) of the Children Act 1989, for the court to exercise its inherent wardship jurisdiction. The court at first instance overruled the parents' refusal. The Court of Appeal allowed the parents' appeal and refused to overrule the parents' decision. They held that the judge at first instance had erred in categorising the mother as unreasonable simply because the clinical evidence was to the effect that the child was a good candidate for a transplant with good prospects of a favourable outcome. The deep rooted concern of the mother was as to the benefits to her son of the major invasive surgery and post-operative treatment, the dangers of failure, long-term as well as short-term, the possibility of the need for further transplants, the likely length of life and the effect upon her of all these concerns. The judge had not, it was held, sufficiently taken into account the relevance or the weight of such considerations in his final balancing exercise. There were broader factors beyond the clinical evidence as to the prospects of success of a transplant to be taken into account. First, the doctor involved and his team while strongly recommending the operation, wished to respect the decision of the mother and were not willing to perform the operation without her consent. Coercing the mother, so to speak, would not assist the child, given the importance of the total co-operation of the mother with the operation and the consequent treatment. Secondly, there were all manner of difficulties in implementing the order with the child and parents abroad – not because the parents would not comply with a court order but because of the disturbance to their lives and the re-adjustments that would be required to have to come back to this country. It was not disputed that the parents were loving and caring parents. Butler-Sloss LJ, at p 510, took the view that 'this mother and this child were one for the purpose of an unusual case'. Whilst it has been suggested that *Re T* places greater weight and emphasis on the parental view, the Court of Appeal made quite clear that each case would turn on its own facts, that the case was unusual and that the test remained the same, namely the paramount consideration was the welfare and best interests of the child.

Downs syndrome

In *Re B (A Minor) (Wardship: Medical Treatment)* [1981] 1 WLR 1421, the parents' refusal to consent to an operation on their baby girl suffering from Downs syndrome was overruled by the Court of Appeal. They held that the operation was to go ahead against the parents' wishes. The parents took the view that the kindest course in their daughter's best interests was for her not to have the operation. The local authority felt she could have a happy and settled home life through long-term fostering or adoption.

Blood transfusions: Jehovah's Witnesses

In *Re S (A Minor) (Medical Treatment)* [1993] 1 FLR 376, the child, aged four and a half years, was diagnosed as suffering from T-cell leukaemia with a high risk of death. His parents were dedicated Jehovah's Witnesses and his family records and instructions had always opposed blood transfusions. The parents were supportive of any form of medical or scientific intervention, provided it did not breach the veto upon the use of blood. The evidence established that either the doctors in whose care the child was had the authority to treat S intensively with the discretion to administer blood, or there was no medical treatment which held any prospect of care for the child. An argument contended on the parents' behalf was that, if the treatment was applied in the face of parental opposition, this would act to the child's detriment in years to come since he would be being parented by parents who believed his life was prolonged by 'an ungodly act'. Thorpe J, as he then was, took the view that such an argument had little foundation in reality and, by his decision, the family were to recognise that responsibility for the consent to the blood transfusion was taken by the court and absolved their conscience of responsibility. Other 'Jehovah's Witnesses cases' involving overruling parental opposition are: *Re E (A Minor)* [1990] 9 BMLR 1; *Re R (A Minor) (Blood Transfusion)* [1993] 2 FLR 757; *Re S (A Minor) (Consent to Medical Treatment)* [1994] 2 FLR 1065 and *Re L (Medical Treatment: Gillick Competency)* [1998] 2 FLR 810.

For legal and medical practitioners involved in any such case (both adults and minors), the handbook entitled *Family Care and Medical Management for Jehovah's Witnesses* sets out in detail the approach of Jehovah's Witnesses, founded on deep religious convictions, to their refusal of blood transfusions, yet their acceptance of most medical and surgical treatments available as well as their willingness to accept alternative treatments to blood transfusions such as 'non-blood expanders'.

8.4   A MINOR'S RIGHTS TO CONSENT TO MEDICAL TREATMENT

8.4.1   A minor's common law right to consent

At common law, a child of sufficient intelligence and understanding (a '*Gillick*-competent' child) can consent to medical treatment, notwithstanding absence of the parents' consent or any express prohibition by them (*Re W (A Minor) (Medical Treatment: Court's Jurisdiction)* [1992] 3 WLR 758 at 764G–H).

In *Gillick v West Norfolk and Wisbech Area Health Authority* [1986] AC 112, the central issue was whether parents could effectively impose a veto on medical treatment for a child patient under the age of 16 years by failing or refusing to consent to treatment to which the child might consent. Mrs Gillick was not challenging the right of a Wardship Court to exercise its parens patriae jurisdiction. She asserted an absolute right of veto on the part of parents generally and herself in particular on medical advice and treatment in relation to their children under the age of 16. The House of Lords decisively rejected her contentions, holding that a child of sufficient intelligence and understanding could consent to medical treatment, notwithstanding any refusal of consent by his or her parents.

The facts of the Gillick case

The case was based on Mrs Victoria Gillick's concern to challenge the legality of a 'Memorandum of Guidance' issued by the Department of Health and Social Security which advised that:

(1) there was a clear need for contraceptive services to be available for, and accessible to, young people at risk of pregnancy irrespective of age;
(2) it was for the doctor to decide whether to provide contraceptive advice and treatment; and
(3) the Medical Defence Union had advised that the parents of a child, of whatever age, independently seeking advice and treatment should not be contacted by any staff without the permission of that child.

None of Mrs Gillick's daughters, then aged 13, 12, 10 and 5, contemplated engaging in sexual intercourse in the immediate future or had sought or were likely independently to seek contraceptive advice or treatment. However, Mrs Gillick, in the absence of assurances she requested, sought declarations that the 'Memorandum of Guidance' was unlawful and against the authority that no doctor was entitled, as a matter of law, to give contraceptive advice and/or abortion advice to any of her children under the age of 16 without her consent.

The Gillick competency test

It was held in the *Gillick* case that a child can consent to treatment on his or her own behalf when he or she achieves a sufficient understanding and intelligence to enable him or her to understand fully what is proposed.

It is a question of fact in each case whether a child seeking advice or 'consenting' to treatment has sufficient understanding of what is involved to give a consent valid in law.

In the case of *Re R (A Minor) (Wardship: Medical Treatment)* [1992] 1 FLR 190, the court was concerned with a minor of 15 years with problems of mental health and disturbed behaviour. The court at first instance and in the Court of Appeal accepted that she lacked the necessary capacity to consent or refuse consent to the proposed treatment. At p 200, Lord Donaldson said:

'But even if she was capable, on a good day, of a sufficient degree of understanding to meet the *Gillick* criteria, her mental disability, to the cure or amelioration of which the proposed treatment was directed, was such that on other days she was not only '*Gillick*-incompetent', but actually sectionable. No child in that situation can be regarded as '*Gillick*-competent' and the Judge was wholly right in so finding in relation to R.'

In *Re K, W and H (Minors) (Medical Treatment)* [1993] 1 FLR 854 at 859, Thorpe J, as he then was, said:

'*Gillick* competency is a developmental concept and will not be lost or acquired on a day to day or week to week basis.'

In *Re W (A Minor) (Medical Treatment: Court Jurisdiction)* [1992] 3 WLR 758, the court was concerned with a girl who had attained 16 years of age and suffered from anorexia nervosa of a serious nature. The Court of Appeal doubted whether the child had sufficient understanding to make the medical choice she had. It was said in the Court of Appeal that 'it is a feature of anorexia nervosa that it is capable of destroying the ability to make an informed choice'.

In *Re L (Medical Treatment: Gillick Competency)* [1998] 2 FLR 810, it was vital for the 14-year-old female patient who had suffered severe burns and was in a life-threatening condition to receive a blood transfusion or transfusions. Her sincere and strong wish was not to have a blood transfusion on the basis of her religious beliefs as a Jehovah's Witness. The President of the Family Division, Sir Stephen Brown, determined, on the evidence, that she was not '*Gillick*-competent', in that she had not been provided with sufficient information as to the grave consequences, including the manner of her death, flowing from her refusal to have been able to make a suitably informed choice. The judge made an order permitting the medical treatment required, despite the fact that L did not consent.

The right of a Gillick-*competent minor to consent to treatment can be overridden by the court*
A minor of any age who is '*Gillick*-competent' in the context of a particular treatment has a right to consent to that treatment, which cannot be overridden by those with parental responsibility, but can be overridden by the court (*Re W* [1992] 3 WLR 758 at 772).

8.4.2 A minor's statutory right to consent

Section 8 of the Family Law Reform Act 1969 gives minors who have attained the age of 16 years a right to consent to surgical, medical or dental treatment. Such a consent cannot be overridden by those with parental responsibility for the minor. It can, however, be overridden by the court.

8.4.3 Donation of organs or blood

Section 8 of the 1969 Act does not extend to permit a minor who has attained 16 years to consent to the donation of organs or blood. The common law right of a minor of any age who is '*Gillick*-competent' to consent to treatment extends to the donation of blood or organs. It is uncontroversial that a *Gillick*-competent minor of any age would be able to consent to give blood under the common law. In relation, however, to so serious a procedure as the donation of an organ by a minor of whatever age, it is most unlikely, for one, or both, of two reasons, that medical practitioners would act solely on the consent of the minor and without the full consent of the minor's parents. First, it would be hard for a doctor to be satisfied that any minor under the age of 18 was *Gillick*-competent in the context of so serious a procedure which could not benefit the child. Secondly, as a matter of ethics and professional duty in respect of the best interests of the minor, it is 'inconceivable', to use the words of Lord Donaldson in *Re W* [1992] 3 WLR 758 at 767:

> 'that he (the doctor) would proceed in reliance solely upon the consent of an underage patient, however *Gillick*-competent in the absence of supporting parental consent . . .'

8.5   A MINOR'S RIGHTS TO REFUSE CONSENT TO MEDICAL TREATMENT

8.5.1   No absolute right of any minor to refuse medical treatment

Unlike an adult, any minor of any age, including one who is '*Gillick*-competent' does not have an absolute right to refuse medical treatment.

8.5.2   The parental right to consent to treatment on behalf of a minor who is refusing treatment

If a minor of any age refuses treatment, a parent or parents, or other person or body with parental responsibility, may consent to such treatment for and on the minor's behalf and thus override the minor's refusal. This applies even if the minor is '*Gillick*-competent'. A parent or parents, or other person or body with parental responsibility, may consent to treatment against the minor's wishes and, as a matter of law, the doctor is then authorised and able to treat the minor according to his or her clinical judgment. In *Re K, W and H (Minors) (Medical Treatment)* [1993] 1 FLR 854, a highly specialised unit for adolescents with disturbed behaviour sought relief from the court under s 8 of the Children Act 1989 in circumstances where three patients had complained about and refused the provision in the unit to them of medication in an emergency. Two of the girls in question were 15 years old and evinced highly disturbed behaviour. The third girl was not quite 15 years old and suffered from mental illness. The parent or parents of each of the three minors consented to the medical treatment provided, including the emergency medication. Thorpe J, as he then was, repeated the principle that where a minor, including one who is *Gillick*-competent refused medical treatment, consent can be given by someone else who has parental responsibility:

'... None of these three is *Gillick*-competent and even if they were *Gillick*-competent it is manifest that their refusal of consent would not expose doctor B ... to the risk of criminal or civil proceedings if he proceeded to administer medication in emergency and in the face of such refusal since in each instance he has a parental consent ...'.

The judge was unwilling to make any orders on the unit's applications and emphasised that applications to the court should be discouraged since it was established that a parental consent would suffice to authorise medical treatment, even if a minor was refusing, as in that case, medication.

Given the principles set out above as to parental consent in the face of a minor's refusal of treatment, 'hair-raising possibilities' were canvassed before the court in *Re W (A Minor) (Medical Treatment: Court's Jurisdiction)* [1992] 3 WLR 758 at 767 as to abortions being carried out by doctors, in reliance upon the consent of parents and despite the refusal of consent by 16- and 17-year-olds. It seems a remote proposition that a doctor would, in these circumstances, be willing to exercise his or her clinical judgment so as to overrule the minor's wishes, notwithstanding the parents' consent. It is to be emphasised that the parental consent, on general principles, only authorises or permits the doctor to treat if he or she sees fit, according to his or her clinical judgment. Lord Donaldson, at p 767 said that:

'Whilst this may be possible as a matter of law, I do not see any likelihood taking account of medical ethics, unless the abortion was truly in the best interests of the child.'

He further said that a safeguard was that:

'the inherent jurisdiction of the court could still be invoked in such a case to prevent an abortion which was contrary to the interests of the minor.'

8.6 THE POWER OF THE COURT TO OVERRULE A MINOR'S REFUSAL OF CONSENT TO TREATMENT

8.6.1 The wide powers of the court to overrule any minor's refusal

In the absence of parental consent or otherwise, the court has power to override, if it sees fit, a refusal to consent to treatment of a minor over 16 years of age, or under that age but *Gillick*-competent (*Re W (A Minor) (Medical Treatment: Court's Jurisdiction)* [1992] 3 WLR 758 at 769):

'There is ample authority for the proposition that the inherent powers of the Court under its parens patriae jurisdiction are theoretically limitless and that they certainly extend beyond the powers of a natural parent ... There can therefore be no doubt that it has power to override the refusal of a minor, whether over the age of sixteen or under that age but "*Gillick*-competent". It does not do so by ordering the doctors to treat which, even if within the Court's powers, would be an abuse of them or by ordering the minor to accept treatment, but by authorising the doctors to treat the minor in accordance with their clinical judgment, subject to any restrictions which the Court may impose.'

8.6.2   The minor's views

The refusal of the minor and his or her age, maturity and understanding and wishes and feelings will weigh importantly:

(a)   in any decision by the parent whether to consent to the treatment, notwithstanding the minor's refusal;
(b)   concerning whether or how the medical practitioner chooses to treat the minor notwithstanding any consent by the parent or court;
(c)   concerning whether the court should grant leave for the treatment to occur against the minor's wishes.

8.6.3   Whether or not the minor lacks capacity

It is axiomatic, in cases of refusal of treatment by minors, that the court will wish to scrutinise whether or not the minor has the capacity to refuse within the requisite test. The test to be applied will be either the '*Gillick*-competency' test or the three-stage test of Thorpe J, as he then was, set out in the case of *Re C (Refusal of Medical Treatment)* [1994] 1 FLR 31. *Re L (Medical Treatment: Gillick Competency)* [1998] 2 FLR 810, concerned a 14-year-old female patient who had suffered severe burns and was in a life-threatening condition. As a Jehovah's Witness, she was refusing consent to a blood transfusion on the grounds of her sincerely held religious beliefs. The court applied the '*Gillick*-competency' test and, for reasons indicated at **8.4.1** in relation to this case, determined her to be not '*Gillick*-competent'. In *A Metropolitan Borough Council v DB* [1997] 1 FLR 767, Cazalet J was concerned with a female minor aged 17 years. She was described as 'a simple soul' with a large number of difficulties. The judge applied the three-stage test of *Re C* and found that she failed each of the three stages.

Consent will be more readily given by the court, it appears, for medical treatment of a minor against his or her wishes, and notwithstanding his or her refusal, if the minor is determined by the court to be lacking in capacity. In *Re R (A Minor) (Wardship: Medical Treatment)* [1992] 1 FLR 190 and in *Re W (A Minor)* [1992] 3 WLR 758, the minors in question were viewed to be lacking in capacity. So also was the case in *Re K, W and H (Minors) (Medical Treatment)* [1993] 1 FLR 854 and in *Re L (Medical Treatment: Gillick Competency)* [1998] 2 FLR 810. In the latter case of *In Re L*, however, the court made clear that, even if the patient was '*Gillick*-competent', the court would still have overridden her refusal to consent to medical treatment since such treatment was determined by the court to be in her best interests.

8.6.4 The 'best interests of the minor' test

Beyond the question of capacity, the court will wish to scrutinise all the evidence and make a decision as to whether it is in the best interests of the minor to overrule his or her refusal to accept treatment. In *Re R (A Minor) (Wardship: Medical Treatment)* [1992] 1 FLR 190, the 15-year-old minor who suffered from disturbed behaviour said she did not want or need the drugs prescribed. Within wardship proceedings, the local authority applied for leave for the unit to administer such medication as was necessary without the girl's consent. The application was granted. In *Re W (A Minor)* [1992] 3 WLR 758, the minor had attained 16 years and was suffering from severe anorexia nervosa. The court held that her best interests required the court to direct her immediate transfer to and treatment at a new unit without her consent.

8.6.5 Power of the court to order the detention of a minor for treatment and the use of reasonable force incidental to treatment

The powers of the court under the inherent jurisdiction are extremely wide and the court will not hesitate to give leave for medical treatment to be effected against the minor's wishes if that is required in the minor's best interests, including authorising the use of force. In the case of *Re C (Detention: Medical Treatment)* [1997] 2 FLR 180, the extent of the court's powers under the inherent jurisdiction was considered by Wall J. The 16-year-old minor suffered from anorexia nervosa. The local authority funded her treatment at a private specialist clinic, yet C absconded from the clinic many times. Her behaviour had become disturbed and suicidal. Doctors at the clinic in question regarded the minor's enforced presence at the clinic under an order of the court as an essential component of her treatment and were not prepared to treat her without such an order. The local authority obtained leave to invoke the court's inherent jurisdiction and sought orders authorising C's detention at the clinic and the administration of medical treatment without her consent. Residence at the clinic was an essential component of her treatment. It was clearly in the minor's best interests to be treated. The court directed that the child should be detained as an in-patient at the clinic for the purposes of medical treatment, using reasonable force if necessary. Notwithstanding that the clinic did not constitute secure accommodation and that, accordingly, the provisions of s 25 of the Children Act 1989 could not apply, detention of the minor against her wishes could be so authorised by the court within the parameters of its inherent jurisdiction. Given the safeguards applying to any order made under s 25 of the Children Act 1989, the court was anxious to provide similar safeguards, and the order provided for C to be discharged from the clinic if the doctors judged that the reasons for her detention no longer applied, and required the clinic to consult with C's parents and the local authority on its treatment plans. It also gave liberty for all parties to apply on short notice to a High Court judge.

In *A Metropolitan Borough Council v DB* [1997] 1 FLR 767, the 17-year-old girl in question, who had a crack cocaine addiction, was in a hospital ward and currently agreeing to necessary treatment. The real concern was that, if she later refused treatment, her condition could deteriorate and a crisis situation could develop which could be fatal if she was not treated within hours. The order made by Cazalet J was in these terms:

> 'Upon it being determined that [the minor] is competent neither to consent to nor to refuse medical treatment, such reasonable force may be authorised by the local authority to be used to implement such medical treatment to [the minor] as may be considered necessary by the doctors concerned for her to prevent her death or serious deterioration in her health.'

The power of the court to override a minor's refusal to submit to medical examination under s 38(6) of the Children Act 1989 and to direct the child to be medically examined, assessed and treated

In *South Glamorgan County Council v W and B* [1993] 1 FLR 574, the court was concerned with a girl aged 15 years. She had long-standing behavioural problems. She had confined herself to the front room of her father's house with curtains drawn for approximately 11 months, and had had hardly any contact with the outside world. The local authority commenced care proceedings. The judge made an interim care order with the direction under s 38(6) of the Children Act 1989 for her to receive psychiatric examination and assessment and, if necessary, to be treated at an adolescent unit and to remain there during assessment. In the event, the minor did not consent to go to the unit. Leave was granted to the local authority under s 100(3) of the 1989 Act to bring proceedings to invoke the exercise of the inherent jurisdiction on the grounds that the result which the local authority wished to achieve could not be so achieved through the making of any order to which s 100(5) applied and there was real cause to believe that, if the inherent jurisdiction of the court was not exercised with respect to the child, she was likely to suffer significant harm. It was held that there was inherent power under the parens patriae jurisdiction to override the refusal of a minor, whether over the age of 16 or under that age, to submit to assessment and medical examination and treatment if it was in her best interests and notwithstanding that she might be of sufficient understanding to make an informed decision about a medical examination or psychiatric examination or assessment. The court further determined that, in an appropriate case where other remedies under the Children Act 1989 had been exhausted and found not to bring about the desired result, there was jurisdiction to resort to other remedies, and the particular remedy was to provide the authority for doctors to treat the child and authority, if it was needed, for the local authority to take all necessary steps to bring the child to the doctors so that she could be assessed and treated properly. On the facts, it was directed that the child should be admitted to the adolescent unit in her own interests without any further delay.

8.7   PRACTICE AND PROCEDURE

8.7.1   Applications under the Children Act 1989

Such applications are governed by Part IV of the FPR 1991. Applications under the 1989 Act in relation to the medical treatment of minors may include, for example, an application for a specific issue order under s 8 where there is a dispute between the parents over proposed medical treatment. Another example is care proceedings initiated by a local authority where, for example, the court is invited to give directions as to a medical or psychiatric or other assessment of the child under the auspices of an interim care order and pursuant to s 38(6) of the Act.

Under r 4.18(1) of the FPR 1991, no person may, without leave of the court, cause the child to be medically or psychiatrically examined, or otherwise assessed, for the purpose of the preparation of expert evidence for use in the proceedings.

8.7.2   Applications under the inherent jurisdiction of the court

The High Court's inherent jurisdiction in relation to children – the parens patriae jurisdiction – is equally exercisable whether the child is or is not a ward of court (*In Re M and N (Minors) (Wardship: Publication of Information)* [1990] Fam 211 at 223G).

As was stated by Balcombe LJ in the case of *Re W (A Minor)* [1992] 3 WLR 758 at 773:

> '... It had long been recognised that wardship was only machinery and the Court's inherent jurisdiction could be exercised whether or not the child was a ward: see, for example, *In Re L (An Infant)* [1968] P 119, 157 ...'.

The inherent jurisdiction is not derivative from the parents' rights and responsibilities but derives from, or is, the delegated performance of the duties of the Crown to protect its subjects, and particularly children, who are the generations of the future (*Re C (A Minor) (Wardship: Medical Treatment) (No 2)* [1990] Fam 39 at 46, [1990] 1 FLR 263 at 266).

In *Re Z (A Minor) (Identification: Restrictions on Publication)* [1997] Fam 1, the Court of Appeal helpfully analysed the High Court's jurisdiction in relation to wardship and the inherent jurisdiction in respect of minors.

In practical terms, the court, when exercising the parens patriae jurisdiction, takes over the rights and duties of the parents. The wishes and views of the parents will be important. However, in the end, the responsibility for the decision will be that of the court alone.

Within its parens patriae jurisdiction, the court will be able to approve or not approve medical treatment for and on behalf of the minor, dependent upon whether such treatment is or is not in the minor's best interests.

The powers of the High Court, under its inherent jurisdiction with respect to minors, are 'theoretically limitless' (*Re W (A Minor) (Medical Treatment: Court's Jurisdiction)* [1992] 3 WLR 758 at 769). To this extent, for example, the court has power to override a minor's refusal to submit to a medical examination directed under s 38(6) of the Children Act 1989 and to direct that the minor is medically examined, assessed or treated.

Proceedings under the inherent jurisdiction are assigned to the Family Division and governed generally by the Rules of the Supreme Court and the FPR 1991. Part V of the FPR 1991 sets out the procedure to be followed when applying for wardship. An application to make a minor a ward of court is made by originating summons in the Family Division, together with an affidavit in support. There is no specific provision made in the FPR 1991 for cases brought under the inherent jurisdiction of the High Court other than in wardship. The appropriate method of commencing proceedings under the inherent jurisdiction other than in wardship is by way of originating summons entitled 'In the Matter of the Inherent Jurisdiction'. To all intents and purposes, however, applications inviting the court to exercise its inherent jurisdiction with respect to minors will normally be made through the machinery of wardship.

The following provisions apply to applications by local authorities for the court to exercise its inherent jurisdiction.

By s 100(3) of the Children Act 1989, a local authority has to seek and obtain leave of the court to be able to apply for the exercise of the court's inherent jurisdiction with respect to children.

By s 100(4) of the Act, the court may only grant leave if it is satisfied that:

(a) the result which the authority wished to achieve could not be achieved through the making of any order of a kind to which subs (5) applies; and
(b) there is reasonable cause to believe that, if the court's inherent jurisdiction is not exercised with respect to the child, he is likely to suffer significant harm.

Section 100(5) applies to any order:

(a) made otherwise than in the exercise of the court's inherent jurisdiction; and
(b) which the local authority is entitled to apply for (assuming, in the case of any application which may only be made with leave, that leave is granted).

8.7.3 Family proceedings in respect of minors to be heard in Chambers

An exception to the basic rule that justice must be administered in public is where the court is exercising its jurisdiction in relation to minors: *Scott v Scott* [1913] AC 417 and *Re G (Adult Patient: Publicity)* [1995] 2 FLR 528.

In cases of special difficulty and sensitivity in which the public interest requires that the court's decision and the reasons for it should be open to public scrutiny, the judge should give judgment in open court, setting out all the relevant facts and the medical and other considerations of which he or she has taken account, but taking all appropriate measures to preserve the personal privacy of those concerned (*Re C (A Minor) (Wardship: Medical Treatment)* [1990] Fam 26 at 37E).

During or following family proceedings, the parents and child may be the subject of publicity, for reasons of celebrity or otherwise. The High Court has a discretion to grant injunctive relief in its inherent jurisdiction, restraining the media from publishing any information calculated to lead to the identification of the child in question, or, indeed, restraining the parents from discussing the child's case with the media. The source and extent of the court's jurisdiction to prevent publicity and the balancing act to be carried out was considered in detail in the case of *In Re Z (A Minor) (Identification: Restrictions on Publication)* [1997] Fam 1 and, more recently, in the case of *In Re G (Minors) (Celebrities: Publicity)* [1999] 1 FLR 409. In the case of *In Re M and N (Minors) (Wardship: Publication of Information)* [1990] Fam 211, Butler-Sloss LJ said at p 223:

> 'The power of the Courts to impose restrictions upon publication for the protection of children is derived from the inherent jurisdiction of the High Court exercising the powers of the Crown as parens patriae. It is not restricted to wardship, which ... is the machinery for its exercise. The sole question is whether the interest of the child should be allowed to prevail over the freedom of the press.'

8.7.4 Next friend: guardian ad litem

In relation to 'specified' proceedings under the Children Act 1989, as defined in s 41 of that Act, the appointment of a guardian ad litem for the child is governed by r 4.10 of the FPR 1991.

In other family proceedings, such as proceedings under the inherent jurisdiction of the High Court in relation to adults and minors and Children Act proceedings in relation to minors other than 'specified' proceedings, the most relevant rule is r 9 of the FPR 1991.

Under r 9.1 of the FPR 1991 a 'person under disability' means a person who is a minor or a patient. A 'patient' means a person who, by reason of mental disorder within the meaning of the Mental Health Act 1983 is incapable of managing and administering his property and affairs.

Rule 9.2(1) of the FPR 1991 provides that, except as otherwise provided, a minor may begin and prosecute any family proceedings only by his next friend and may defend the proceedings only by his guardian ad litem.

However, r 9.2A of the FPR 1991 provides that, in certain circumstances, a minor may begin, prosecute or defend proceedings under the Children Act 1989 or the inherent jurisdiction of the High Court with respect to minors, without a next friend or guardian ad litem.

Rule 9.2A(1) of the FPR 1991 allows a minor to prosecute or defend proceedings without a next friend or guardian:

'(a)   where he has obtained leave of the court for that purpose; or
(b)   where a solicitor—
     (i)   considers that the minor is able, having regard to his understanding, to give instructions in relation to the proceedings; and
     (ii)   has accepted instructions from the minor to act for him in the proceedings and, where the proceedings have begun, is so acting.'

Under r 9.2A(4) of the FPR 1991, where a minor has a next friend or guardian ad litem in proceedings and wishes to prosecute or defend the remaining stages of the proceedings without a next friend or guardian ad litem, the minor may apply to the court for leave for that purpose and for the removal of the next friend or guardian ad litem. In *Re W (A Minor) (Medical Treatment: Court's Jurisdiction)* [1992] 3 WLR 758, the minor who was 16, had as her guardian ad litem the Official Solicitor, but was able to dispense with representation by the Official Solicitor and instruct her own legal representatives.

8.8   THE UNBORN CHILD

The legal status of the unborn child has arisen and been considered in the courts in differing applications and circumstances.

8.8.1   Applications by a father to prevent a mother having an abortion

In *Paton v The British Pregnancy Advisory Service Trustees* [1979] QB 276, a father made an unsuccessful attempt to obtain an injunction in the High Court to prevent his wife having an abortion. It was held that the foetus, in English law, does not have a right of its own, at least until it is born and does not have a separate existence from its mother until it is born.

In *C v S and Another* [1987] 2 FLR 505, a High Court judge refused relief to an unborn child on that occasion named as the 'second plaintiff', in an attempt by the father to prevent the mother having an abortion. The judge referred to a number of decisions in Canada stating that an unborn child was not a person and any rights accorded to the foetus were held contingent upon its subsequent birth alive.

8.8.2   Applications toward an unborn child

In *Re F (In Utero) (Wardship)* [1988] 2 FLR 307, a local authority attempted to make the unborn child of a mentally disturbed mother a ward of court. The Court of Appeal upheld the judge at first instance, in determining that the court did not have power to ward a foetus. Balcombe LJ, in his judgment, considered s 1 of the Infant Life (Preservation) Act 1929 and Article 2 of the European Convention for the Protection of Human Rights and Fundamental Freedoms 1950 and found that neither supported the local authority on the issue of the wardship of the unborn child. He said, at p 325C:

'Approaching the question as one of principle, in my judgmen jurisdiction to make an unborn child a ward of court. Since an unbori hypothesi, no existence independent of its mother, the only purpose of jurisdiction to include a foetus is to enable the mother's actions to b controlled. Indeed that is the purpose of the present application.'

8.8.3 The interests of the unborn child where the mother refuses medical intervention

Where a pregnant mother is determined by the court, as in *Re MB (Medical Treatment)* [1997] 2 FLR 426, to be not competent, medical intervention will occur in the best interests of the adult patient and consequently the interests of the unborn child will be protected.

Two cases have considered at length the position in law of the unborn child. In both, the mothers required Caesarean operations. In *Re MB (Medical Treatment)*, the mother was agreeable to a Caesarean operation but, at the last moment, was overwhelmed by a fear of needles and withdrew her consent to the operation. Without the anaesthetic, the Caesarean operation could not occur. A declaration was granted that it would be lawful for the consultant in question to operate on her using reasonable force if necessary. The Court of Appeal held that, at the time of her refusal, the patient was temporarily incompetent. The Court of Appeal considered at length the status of the unborn child:

> 'The law is, in our judgment, clear that a competent woman who has the capacity to decide may, for religious reasons, other reasons, or for no reasons at all, choose not to have medical intervention, even though, as we have already stated, the consequence may be the death or serious handicap of the child she bears or her own death. She may refuse to consent to the anaesthesia injection in the full knowledge that her decision may significantly reduce the chance of her unborn child being born alive. The foetus up to the moment of birth does not have any separate interests capable of being taken into account when a court has to consider an application for a declaration in respect of a Caesarean section operation. The court does not have the jurisdiction to declare that such medical intervention is lawful to protect the interests of the unborn child even at the point of birth.'

In *St George's Healthcare NHS Trust v S* [1998] 2 FLR 728, the mother, a veterinary nurse, wanted a natural birth. She underwent no ante-natal care. At 36 weeks of her pregnancy she was found to be suffering from pre-eclampsia and was advised that she needed to be admitted to hospital for an induced delivery and that, without such treatment, her health and life and the life of her baby were in danger. She fully understood the potential risks but rejected the advice. She was admitted to hospital against her will. A judge was asked to and did grant a declaration dispensing with her consent to treatment and, thereafter, her baby was born by Caesarean section. She applied to the Court of Appeal, who allowed her appeal, holding that, as a competent adult at the time, her refusal of treatment was fully justified on the grounds of her right of self-determination and should not have been overridden, notwithstanding that such refusal jeopardised the life not only of herself but also that of her unborn child. In relation to the status of the unborn child and protection to be afforded to it, at p 746 of that authority, the Court of Appeal summarised the position as follows:

> 'In our judgment while pregnancy increases the personal responsibilities of a woman it does not diminish her entitlement to decide whether or not to undergo medical treatment. Although human, and protected by the law in a number of different ways set out in the judgment in *Re MB*, an unborn child is not a separate person from its mother. Its need for medical assistance does not prevail over her rights. She is entitled not to be forced to submit to an invasion of her body against her will, whether her own life or that of her unborn child depends on it. Her right is not reduced or diminished merely because her decision to exercise it may appear morally repugnant. The declaration in this case involved the removal of the baby from within the body of her mother under physical compulsion. Unless lawfully justified this constituted an infringement of the mother's autonomy. Of themselves the perceived needs of the foetus did not provide the necessary justification.'

8.9   MEDICAL EXAMINATIONS AND INTERVIEWS OF MINORS

8.9.1   Medical examinations prior to or in the absence of legal proceedings

The position in law commensurate with the principles set out in this chapter on consent is that, save in exceptional circumstances, such as an emergency, no doctor may examine an immature minor without the consent of a parent or parents, or other person or body with parental responsibility. Where a full care order has been made in respect of an immature minor and there are no continuing legal proceedings, consent to a medical examination of the immature minor will be sought of the local authority who exercise parental responsibility for the minor. If the minor has sufficient understanding to meet the criteria of the '*Gillick* test', he or she may consent to an examination on his or her own behalf.

8.9.2   Medical examinations during the currency of family proceedings

If family proceedings are instituted, permission must be sought from the court before any further proposed medical examination of the subject child or children may occur.

Under r 4.18(1) of the FPR 1991:

> 'no person may, without the leave of the Court, cause the child to be medically or psychiatrically examined, or otherwise assessed, for the purpose of the preparation of expert evidence for use in the proceedings.'

It is necessary to scrutinise succinctly the provisions as to medical or psychiatric examination of children in 'public law' cases. By s 44(6)(b) of the Children Act

1989, where the court makes an emergency protection order, it may give such directions (if any) as it considers appropriate with respect to the medical or psychiatric examination or other assessment of the child.

Under s 44(8) of the Act, a direction under subs (6)(b) may be to the effect that there is to be:

(a) no such examination or assessment; or
(b) no such examination or assessment unless the court directs otherwise.

Where a direction is given by the court for the medical or psychiatric examination of a child, the child may, by s 44(7) of the Act, refuse to submit to the examination or other assessment if he or she is of sufficient understanding to make an informed decision.

When the court makes an interim care order or interim supervision order under s 38 of the Children Act 1989, or, at any time while such an order is in force, the court may give such directions, if any, as it considers appropriate with regard to the medical or psychiatric examination or other assessment of the child, but if the child is of sufficient understanding to make an informed decision, he or she may refuse to submit to the examination or other assessment: s 38(6) of the Children Act 1989.

By s 38(7) of the Act, a direction under s 38(6) may be to the effect that there is to be either no such examination or assessment, or no such examination or assessment unless the court directs otherwise.

8.9.3 Medical examinations and interviews of minors in respect of allegations of sexual abuse

The principles of law already referred to are equally applicable where such allegations are made as are the effect of the FPR 1991 if Children Act 1989 proceedings have been instituted.

The Report of the Inquiry into Child Abuse in Cleveland 1987 remains the touchstone for practice and procedure in this field and, since then, procedures have been developed involving cooperation between agencies in investigating allegations of sexual abuse in respect of minors.

The report of a working party of the Royal College of Physicians entitled 'Physical signs of sexual abuse in children', now in its second edition, published in 1997, is, and has been, widely used by the legal profession, the medical profession and within the courts.

In respect of issues raised in relation to consents to medical examination, practitioners are referred to Chapter 11 of the Cleveland Report and, in particular, to paras 11.31 to 11.40.

Assuming an appropriate consent has been forthcoming, medical practitioners who have examined a minor for suspected sexual abuse and disagree in their findings and conclusions should discuss their reports and resolve their differences, where possible, and, in the absence of agreement, should identify the areas of dispute between them, recognising that their purpose is to act in the best interests of the child: see 6.f at p 248 of the Cleveland Report under the heading 'Recommendations to the Medical Profession'.

In the case of *Re D (Child Abuse: Interviews)* [1998] 2 FLR 10, the Court of Appeal reviewed the practice to be adopted in interviewing children where allegations of sexual abuse are made. The thrust of the decision was to confirm again that social workers and medical and other health professionals should be on guard against prompting or leading children to provide information in these cases. The court referred to the detailed recommendations in chapter 12 of the Cleveland Report and subsequent decisions of the Court of Appeal and the Family Division in this regard, together with the principles laid down in the Memorandum of Good Practice. The Court of Appeal determined that, for the purposes of civil proceedings in the family context, the guidelines set out in the Memorandum, required for criminal trials, may not have to be strictly adhered to, but its underlying principles are equally applicable to care or private family law cases. It was reiterated in the judgment of Butler-Sloss LJ that spontaneous information provided by a child is obviously more valuable than information fed to the child by leading questions or prompting. Whilst some children have to be helped to give evidence, the greater the help provided by facilitating the answers, the less reliable the answers will be. Legal practitioners advising in this field and medical practitioners and social workers involved in the difficult task of questioning young children where allegations of sexual abuse arise will be well served by considering carefully the full judgment of the Court of Appeal in this case.

Chapter 9

ADVANCE STATEMENTS OR 'LIVING WILLS'

9.1 THE NATURE AND PURPOSE OF ADVANCE STATEMENTS OR 'LIVING WILLS'

A person who is over 18 years old and competent may express in advance how he or she wishes to be medically treated if he or she becomes incompetent. This is described as an advance statement or, more commonly, a 'living will'. Through advance statements, adults may, for example, decline in advance specific treatment, including life-sustaining treatment.

An advance statement is often used as a way in which an adult may refuse in advance any particular medical treatments or procedures. This is described as an advance refusal of treatment, which is a type or part of an advance statement. It may also be described as an advance directive. It is particularly relevant in a legal sense, since such a refusal will be taken into account and weighed by the court and may indeed be binding in the event of a dispute as to the medical treatment of a patient.

Patients and doctors, of course, often discuss in advance how the predictable stages of an illness should be managed in order to reflect the patients' own wishes and values. Advanced discussion and decision-making are particularly important where there is a likelihood of the patient's mental capacity becoming impaired.

The House of Lords Select Committee on Medical Ethics in 1994 favoured the encouragement of advance statements as a way of extending choice for patients in relation to medical treatment. The Select Committee called for a Code of Practice on advance statements for health professionals. From this, there is now the British Medical Association Code of Practice of April 1995, entitled 'Advance Statements About Medical Treatment'.

The Code gives guidance to health professionals as to the nature, effects and purposes of advance statements or 'living wills' by patients concerning their future medical treatment. A copy of the Code of Practice is enclosed within the Appendix.

It is important to make clear that the Code expressly does not address euthanasia, which is a matter entirely separate from and outside the ambit of advance statements.

As is stated in the BMA views on advance statements issued in November 1992 and revised in May 1995, the fundamental aim of the advance statement is to provide a means for the patient to continue to exercise autonomy and shape the end of his or her life.

9.2   THE ABSENCE OF STATUTORY PROVISION IN RELATION TO ADVANCE STATEMENTS OR 'LIVING WILLS'

An advance statement or 'living will' does not, as yet, have the status or enforceability of a conventional will, yet a part of its provisions may have legal force. Nor, currently, is there any statutory provision as to advance statements, yet the Law Commission has proposed in its report on Mental Incapacity (Law Com No 231) that there should be legislation to incorporate the statutory recognition of advance refusals of treatment. In the absence of such statutory provision, the Code of Practice of the BMA is an important document for consideration, not only by health professionals but also legal practitioners, who may be dealing with a case concerning advance statements or advising a client accordingly.

9.3   THE CONTENTS OF ADVANCE STATEMENTS OR 'LIVING WILLS' AND THEIR EFFECT

9.3.1   Statements of general beliefs and preferences in relation to medical treatment

An advance statement may comprise or include a 'requesting' statement reflecting an individual's aspirations and preferences in relation to medical treatment. This can help health professionals identify how the person would like to be treated without binding them to that course of action, if it conflicts with professional judgment. An advance statement may comprise or include a statement of the general beliefs and aspects of life which an individual values.

Such a statement may make no specific request or refusal, but attempt to give a biographical portrait of the individual as an aid for medical practitioners in deciding what he or she would want in relation to medical treatment.

9.3.2   Statements declining in advance life-sustaining treatment in certain circumstances

An advance statement may comprise or include a statement which, rather than refusing any particular treatment, specifies a degree of irreversible deterioration (such as a diagnosis of PVS) after which no life-sustaining treatment should be given. Such a statement is capable of having legal force.

9.3.3   Statements refusing in advance a particular treatment or treatments

That part of an advance statement which constitutes a clear refusal in advance of particular treatment or treatments by an adult who is competent and understands the implications of that decision will have the same legal force as a contemporaneous refusal made by a competent adult patient to a medical practitioner. In *Airedale NHS Trust v Bland* [1993] AC 789, HL, the House of Lords expressed how, in relation to medical treatment, medical practitioners were bound to respect the decision of a competent adult patient refusing or declining medical treatment, even though such a refusal was adjudged to be not in the best interests of the patient. That such a refusal is binding is commensurate with the principle of self-determination and autonomy of the individual patient. A doctor's duty to act in the best interests of the patient will, accordingly, be qualified where the doctor does not adjudge the patient's refusal to be in his or her best interests. Nevertheless, such a refusal by a competent adult will be binding, however detrimental the consequences to him or her.

In relation to advance refusals of treatment, Lord Goff, at p 864 in the *Bland* case, said as follows:

> 'Moreover the same principle applies where the patient's refusal to give his consent has been expressed at an earlier date, before he became unconscious or otherwise incapable of communicating it; though in such circumstances special care may be necessary to ensure that the prior refusal of consent is still properly to be regarded as applicable in the circumstances which have subsequently occurred ...'

In *Re T (An Adult) (Consent to Medical Treatment)* [1992] 2 FLR 458, a female adult patient who had a 'Jehovah's Witness background' was in hospital and indicated verbally that she did not wish to have a blood transfusion. She thereafter signed a hospital form refusing consent to a blood transfusion. Such a form was simply a pro forma document designed to protect the hospital from liability. The medical staff were abiding by the patient's refusal and, in circumstances where her condition was deteriorating, her father applied to the courts seeking the authorisation of a blood transfusion for her.

In the Court of Appeal, it was held that the patient's refusal was not valid and was vitiated by a number of factors, including the patient's mother's possibly undue influence on her, her fatigue and confusion and the lack of explanation given to her when she signed the form as to the full implications of such refusal if she became very seriously ill. At the time that she signed the form refusing consent, there was discussion by staff with her as to alternative options for treatment that might be available other than a blood transfusion. Lord Donaldson, in his judgment in the Court of Appeal, makes clear that a refusal of medical treatment can take the form of a declaration of intention never to consent in the future or never to consent in some future circumstances. Such an anticipatory choice, he indicates, will be binding if clearly established and applicable in the circumstances.

Where an adult has made her advance refusal of treatment and thereafter becomes seriously ill, three important factors, accordingly, arise as to the advance refusal and its effect. First, the advance refusal must have been made when the adult was competent. Secondly, the advance refusal must be clearly established. Thirdly, care is necessary to ensure that the advance or prior refusal of consent is still properly to be regarded as applicable in the circumstances which have subsequently occurred.

In *Re C (Refusal of Medical Treatment)* [1994] 1 FLR 31, the adult patient had repeatedly insisted that he was unwilling to have his leg amputated, notwithstanding the advice of the consultant in question that such treatment was necessary. The patient was suffering from gangrene in the leg. His refusal of the proposed treatment was expressed to the hospital, both orally by himself and in writing through correspondence by his solicitors. They sought assurances from the hospital that no such treatment would in the future be effected, namely amputation of the leg without the patient's express consent. In the absence of such assurances being given, the patient applied by originating summons for a declaration to the effect that his wishes and refusal as to the medical treatment proposed should be respected and upheld. Thorpe J, as he then was, held that, notwithstanding his mental illness and background, the patient was capable of deciding the issue in question and, whether or not such a decision was to be viewed as reasonable, the patient's refusal should be upheld and respected. The court was, he held, entitled to exercise its inherent jurisdiction to determine the effect of a purported advance directive as to future medical treatment. Importantly, therefore, the relief granted by the court, by injunction or declaration, could extend beyond present to future circumstances.

9.3.4   Advance medical directives of Jehovah's Witnesses in relation to blood transfusions

A specimen of an advance medical directive is reproduced in Part III of this book.

An advance refusal of treatment, such as a blood transfusion, by an adult of sound mind, must be respected and will be upheld if it is clearly established and applicable to the circumstances which have arisen. Medical practitioners must also always be alert to any suggestion that an advance refusal has been altered or withdrawn.

In relation to minors, however, in the absence of parental consent or otherwise, the court has power to override a minor's refusal of treatment, such as a blood transfusion, and in whatever form the refusal presents itself if such treatment is determined by the court to be in the minor's best interests. In *Re L (Medical Treatment: Gillick Competency)* [1998] 2 FLR 810, the female patient, aged 14, who was a Jehovah's Witness had herself signed 'An Advance Medical Directive/Release' form in which she expressed her view and wish that she should not be given blood if she sustained injury. Her views were sincere and founded on deeply held religious beliefs. She had suffered severe burns and was in a life-threatening condition. The medical evidence indicated that she required a blood transfusion or transfusions. It was an extreme case and her position was grave. The judge gave leave for the proposed treatment under the inherent jurisdiction of the High Court, as being in her best interests, notwithstanding that she did not consent. The court determined that she was not '*Gillick*-competent', but even if she were, in her best interests, her refusal would still be overriden.

9.3.5 Nomination of a consultee or healthcare proxy

Paragraph 2 of the definitions section of the Code of Practice of the BMA on advance statements indicates that an advance statement may name another person who should be consulted at the time a medical decision is made. It is important to emphasise here that no one including a relative may consent to or refuse treatment on behalf of an incompetent adult. The views of the proxy or nominated person cannot be binding on the medical practitioners involved, yet it is at the heart of good practice for there to be consultation between the doctor and his team and the patient's family and/or next of kin. The nomination of a consultee or healthcare proxy will allow his or her views to be sought and considered with a view to confirming the patient's intention or wishes in cases of doubt or otherwise. The closest the court has come to considering the position of a healthcare proxy – although it was not expressed as such – is in the case of *Re S (Hospital Patient: Court's Jurisdiction)* [1995] 1 FLR 1075.

9.4 THE FORM OF AN ADVANCE STATEMENT OR 'LIVING WILL'

The BMA has maintained that any clear and coherent statement by an informed patient may suffice and that it is not necessary to adopt a particular form of words. An advance statement or 'living will', accordingly, can be a witnessed oral statement, a written document, a signed printed card, a smart card or a note of a discussion recorded in a patient's file. A number of forms of living will have been produced by various organisations. By way of example, a copy of the 'living will' produced by the Terrence Higgins Trust is set out Part III with the kind permission of the Trust and King's College, London, in both of whom copyright resides. Alternate and varying precedents may be found in a book by Denzil Lush, Master of the Court of Protection, entitled *Elderly Clients: A Precedent Manual* (Jordans, 1996).

It is consistently advised that patients who draft advance statements or living wills should do so with the benefit of medical advice. It is also advisable that the completed advance statement or 'living will' is witnessed and signed by a third party.

The onus for ensuring that the advance statement or living will is appropriately drafted and available lies with the patient. The BMA has suggested that patients who have drafted an advance statement carry a card indicating the fact as well as lodging a copy with their doctor.

9.5 SAFEGUARDS ATTACHING TO ADVANCE STATEMENTS OR 'LIVING WILLS'

Patients cannot use advance statements to insist on the provision of certain treatments, but they may authorise or refuse treatments. Advance statements or living wills do not apply to those persons who have not attained the age of 18 years.

The Code of Practice provides that as a matter of policy people should not be able to refuse basic care in advance, or instruct others to refuse it on their behalf. Basic care is to provide comfort to the patient and to alleviate his or her pain, symptoms or distress. The exact ambit of 'basic care' is uncertain. The Draft Bill proposed by the Law Commission and attached to its report on Mental Incapacity (No 231) contains provision at cl 9 for advance refusals of treatment. Clause 9(7) states that an advance refusal of treatment shall not preclude the provision for the person who made it of basic care and thereafter in cl 9(8) defines 'basic care' as meaning care to maintain bodily cleanliness and to alleviate severe pain and the provision of direct oral nutrition and hydration.

Clause 9(6) of the Draft Bill provides that an advance refusal of treatment may, at any time, be withdrawn or altered by the person who made it, if he then has the capacity to do so. Leaving aside the Draft Bill, a competent adult must always be able to review and override a previous refusal. Since it is strongly recommended that patients who draft advance statements should do so with the benefit of medical advice, patients are encouraged to review their advance statements at regular intervals and to indicate the document's continuing validity by a date stamp or sticker.

Where, at the crucial time of serious illness, there is controversy over the validity or applicability of an advance refusal or whether it has been withdrawn or attached, a doctor will be entitled to take action to prevent the patient's death or a serious deterioration in his or her condition, pending a decision from the court. Such a provision is set out in cl 9(7)(b) of the Draft Bill of the Law Commission. At common law, the principle of necessity permits a doctor to act and provide medical treatment in an emergency without the consent of the patient.

Chapter 10

MEDICAL TREATMENT OTHER THAN FOR PURELY MEDICAL REASONS

10.1 STERILISATION

10.1.1 Prior sanction of the High Court required

There is, understandably, concern and anxiety in relation to proposed sterilisation operations on either minors or mentally incapacitated adults. Such an operation involves the deprivation of a woman's basic human right to reproduce. A major concern has been to be vigilant that a sterilisation operation should not occur for any reasons of convenience in relation to a minor or adult who is difficult to care for.

Sterilisation of a girl under 18 should only be carried out with the leave of a High Court judge: *Re B (A Minor) (Wardship: Sterilisation)* [1988] 1 AC 199, HL.

In relation to adults, a sterilisation operation should never be carried out upon a woman incapable of giving her own consent, unless there has been prior approval of a High Court judge that the procedure was one which was in the best interests of the woman: *Re S (Medical Treatment: Adult Sterilisation)* [1998] 1 FLR 944.

10.1.2 The special features of a sterilisation operation

The operation will in most cases be irreversible. By reason of the general irreversibility of the operation, the almost certain result of it will be to deprive the woman concerned of what is widely and properly regarded as one of the fundamental rights of a woman, namely, the right to bear children. The deprivation of that right gives rise to moral and emotional considerations to which many people attach great importance.

If the question whether the operation is in the best interests of the adult or minor is left to be decided without the involvement of the court, there may be a greater risk of it being decided wrongly or at least of it being thought to have been decided wrongly. If there is no involvement of the court, there is a risk of the operation being carried out for improper reasons or with improper motives. The involvement of the court in the decision to operate, if that is the decision reached, will serve to protect the doctor or doctors who performed the operation and any others who may be concerned in it from subsequent adverse criticism or claims.

Lord Griffiths, in the case of *Re F (Mental Patient: Sterilisation)* [1990] AC 1, HL, at 68, summarised the reason for the caution and concern in relation to these operations as follows:

> '... The argument in this appeal has ranged far and wide in search of a measure to protect those who cannot protect themselves from the insult of an unnecessary sterilisation. Every judge who has considered the problem has recognised that there should be some control mechanism imposed upon those who have the care of infants or mentally incompetent women of child bearing age to prevent or at least inhibit them from sterilising the women without approval of the High Court. I am, I should make clear, speaking now and hereafter of an operation for sterilisation which is proposed not for the treatment of diseased organs but an operation on a woman with healthy reproductive organs in order to avoid the risk of pregnancy. The reasons for the anxiety about a sterilisation which it is proposed should be carried out for other than purely medical reasons, such as the removal of the ovaries to prevent the spread of cancer, are readily understandable and are shared throughout the common law world.'

10.1.3 Minors and sterilisation

It is helpful to contrast two cases involving the sterilisation of minors.

In the case of *In Re D (A Minor) (Wardship: Sterilisation)* [1976] 2 WLR 279, the girl involved, D, was aged 11 years and suffering from an unusual syndrome of which the symptoms were accelerated growth during infancy, epilepsy, general clumsiness and emotional instability, as well as an impairment of mental function. She had, however, a dull normal intelligence and her clumsiness was lessening and her behaviour was improving. It was not possible to predict her future role in society, but the likelihood was that she would have sufficient capacity to marry. Her widowed mother, worried in case D might give birth to a baby which she was incapable of caring for and which might also be abnormal, wanted D to be sterilised. The consultant paediatrician, under whose care D was, recommended a sterilisation operation and a consultant gynaecologist agreed to perform it. Certain persons concerned with D's welfare, including the plaintiff, an educational psychologist, challenged the decision to operate. In the case of D, it was left to the educational psychologist as plaintiff to apply to make D a ward of court. The Official Solicitor was appointed as D's guardian ad litem at the plaintiff's request. It was held that the court would not risk the incurring of damage which it could not repair but would rather prevent the damage being done; the operation could be delayed or prevented if D were to remain a ward of court and, accordingly, the court should exercise its protective functions in regard to D and continue her wardship. The judge took the view that a decision to perform an operation, such as that proposed, for non-therapeutic purposes on a minor could not be within a doctor's sole clinical judgment.

The facts of *In Re B (A Minor) (Wardship: Sterilisation)* [1988] 1 AC 199 are very different. B, a girl aged 17 years, suffered from a moderate degree of mental handicap but had a very limited intellectual development. Although 17, her ability to understand speech was that of a six-year-old and her ability to express herself was that of a two-year-old. Her mother and staff at the council residential institution where she lived became aware that she was beginning to show signs of sexual awareness, exemplified by provocative approaches to male members of staff and other residents. The local authority applied by originating summons for an order making B a ward of court and for leave to be given for her to undergo a sterilisation operation. Evidence was adduced that B could not be placed on any effective contraceptive regime and that she was not capable of knowing the causal connection between intercourse and childbirth, the nature of pregnancy or what was involved in delivery. She would panic and require heavy sedation during a normal delivery, which carried the risk of injury to the child, and delivery by Caesarean section was deemed to be inappropriate as there was the likelihood of B opening up her post-operative wounds, thus preventing the healing of the scar. She had no maternal instincts and was unlikely ever to desire or be able to care for a child. The judge at first instance gave leave for the operation to be carried out. The Official Solicitor, as guardian ad litem, appealed to the Court of Appeal. The Court of Appeal dismissed the appeal, thereby endorsing that the operation should be carried out as being in her best interests. It was held that a court, exercising wardship jurisdiction, when reaching a decision on an application to authorise an operation for the sterilisation of the ward, was concerned with only one primary and paramount consideration, namely the welfare and best interests of the ward. The conclusion of the Court of Appeal was that, on the totality of the evidence, the operation would be in the patient's best interests.

10.1.4   Adults and sterilisation

It is an obvious point, yet nevertheless important to emphasise, that the court will have different facts, and, perhaps, different considerations, in each particular case of this nature that comes before it. Accordingly, the court will in each and every case of this nature carefully and exhaustively examine the evidence presented.

In the case of *Re LC (Medical Treatment: Sterilisation)* [1997] 2 FLR 258, the judge at first instance indicated that, both on the wider implications of the question of whether a severely handicapped person should be subjected to non-consensual invasive surgery, and on the facts of the individual case, the balance could be argued one way or another. In the end, his decision was based, understandably in the circumstances, on very practical and pragmatic considerations. The patient was mentally handicapped with an intellectual age of about three and a half. She was born in 1972. In 1991, in the care of a residential home, she was indecently assaulted by a member of staff. She had thereafter been moved to another home with an infinitely superior standard of care. It was a small home with dedicated staff. The local authority, supported by the mother of the patient, contended that the patient was vulnerable in the future to the possibility of sexual abuse, the risk of which could not be eliminated and hence it would be in her best interests for the court to sanction the proposed sterilisation operation. The Official Solicitor, as well as a key social worker, held the view that such an operation was not in the patient's best interests. The judge held that the evidence established that the level of care at the home now was of such exceptionally high quality that, whilst it continued, it would not be in the patient's best interests to impose upon her the surgical procedure, which was not without risks or painful consequences. Accordingly, no order was made on the originating summons.

In the case of *Re X (Adult Sterilisation)* [1998] 2 FLR 1124, however, the conclusion of the court on the evidence before it was that permanent sterilisation was in the best interests of the patient. The patient X was 31 years of age, physically able but severely mentally retarded. She regularly attended an adult training centre and appeared to enjoy physical contact with men. She had a particularly close relationship with one male user of the centre. She had been fitted with a contraceptive coil but when that needed to be replaced, X's parents, supported by the Official Solicitor, sought and obtained declaratory relief on the basis that permanent sterilisation involving only one operation was in X's best interests. There was a real risk that X would have a sexual relationship and might become pregnant. Although X said she would like a baby, she was incapable of caring for a child whose birth and inevitable removal from her would be frightening and upsetting to her. Some reliable form of contraception was therefore essential to prevent the psychological damage which would probably result from pregnancy. The only realistic alternative to sterilisation was the contraceptive coil which, because it would need to be replaced regularly, would involve three further operations and the risk of infection.

In the case of *Re F* [1990] 2 AC 1, the view of the judge at first instance was confirmed in both the Court of Appeal and the House of Lords that a sterilisation was in the best interests of the patient. F was a 36-year-old, mentally handicapped woman residing in a mental hospital and with the mental age of a small child. The question of her being sterilised had arisen because of a relationship which she had formed with a male patient at the same hospital. The relationship was of a sexual nature and probably involved sexual intercourse, or something close to it, about twice a month. The relationship was entirely voluntary on the patient's part and it was likely that she obtained pleasure from it. There was no reason to believe that she had other than the ordinary fertility of a woman of her age. Because of her mental disability, however, she could not have coped at all with pregnancy, labour or delivery, the meaning of which she would not have understood. Nor could she have cared for a baby, if she had ever had one. In those circumstances, it would have been, on the evidence, from a psychiatric point of view, disastrous for her to conceive a child. There was a serious objection to each of the ordinary methods of contraception. So far as the varieties of the pill were concerned, she would not have been able to have used them effectively, and there was a risk of their causing damage to her physical health. So far as an intra-uterine device was concerned, there would be danger of infection arising, the symptoms of which she would not have been able to describe so that remedial measures could not have been taken in time. It was in those circumstances, and upon such evidence, that the court concluded the sterilisation operation to be in F's best interests.

Whereas in the above case of *Re F* the patient had formed a sexual relationship with someone else, in the case of *Re S (Medical Treatment: Adult Sterilisation)* [1998] 1 FLR 944, the essential issue for the court was the risk in the future of the patient being 'sexually exploited'. The patient S was 22. She was described by the judge as a charming and attractive young woman and, to all outward appearances, entirely normal. However, her mental and emotional state was such that she was quite unable to look after herself. She had virtually no ability to communicate, except by making some very basic noises. She required help in dressing and looking after her own basic physical needs. She could not be left to walk alone along a street. More particularly, she had no understanding of sexuality. The patient's mother sought a declaration that it would be lawful for her daughter to be sterilised to eliminate the risk of pregnancy. The issue before the court was whether the risk of pregnancy was such as to require sterilisation, with the consequent imposition on S of necessary invasive procedures which carried a risk of fatality. The assessment of the future risk involved a degree of speculation which had to be based on circumstances that existed, or could be reasonably foreseen to exist. In the absence of any identifiable, rather than speculative risk, the court adjudged that the mother's application should be refused. Importantly, the thrust of the submission made on behalf of the Official Solicitor was that, if, in the circumstances of the case of *Re S*, the court was to declare sterilisation to be lawful, then it would be difficult to envisage any factual situation in which the relief would be refused.

10.1.5   Practice and procedure in relation to sterilisation

Minors
The Practice Note of the Official Solicitor on sterilisation of June 1996 [1996] 2 FLR 111, is set out in Part III.

Applications in respect of a minor should be made in the Family Division of the High Court within either proceedings under the inherent jurisdiction of the High Court or an application under the Children Act 1989 for a specific issue order under s 8(1). The preferred course is to apply within the court's inherent jurisdiction.

The plaintiff or applicant should normally be a parent or one of those responsible for the care of the patient, or those intending to carry out the proposed operation. The patient must always be a party and should normally be a defendant or respondent. In cases in which the patient is defendant, the patient's guardian ad litem should normally be the Official Solicitor. In any case in which the Official Solicitor does not represent the patient, he should be a defendant.

The purpose of the proceedings will be to establish whether or not the proposed sterilisation is in the best interests of the minor. There will, in every case, be a hearing before a High Court judge fixed for directions on the first open date after the passage of eight weeks from the issue of the originating summons.

A court exercising the wardship jurisdiction is the only authority empowered to authorise such a drastic step as sterilisation on a minor after a full and informed investigation. A doctor performing a sterilisation operation with the consent of the parents but without the approval of the High Court might still be liable in criminal, civil or professional proceedings.

In relation to minors, applicants should seek an order in the following or a broadly similar form:

> 'It is ordered that there be leave to perform an operation of sterilisation on the minor and to carry out such post-operative treatment and care as may be necessary in her best interests.'

Adults

The Practice Note of the Official Solicitor on sterilisation of June 1996 is reproduced in Part III of this book.

The jurisdiction for the court to consider a proposed sterilisation operation upon an incompetent adult is different to that of a minor. In the absence of parens patriae jurisdiction for incompetent adults, the court has jurisdiction to consider whether a proposed operation or other medical treatment upon an incompetent adult is lawful as being in his or her best interests. Such a distinction is evidenced by the wording and type of relief sought in this regard in relation to an incompetent adult. Applications in respect of an adult should be by way of originating summons in the Family Division of the High Court for an order in the following or broadly similar form:

> 'It is declared that the operation of sterilisation proposed to be performed on (specified adult) being in the existing circumstances in her best interests can lawfully be performed on her despite her inability to consent to it.
> It is ordered that in the event of a material change in the existing circumstances occurring before the said operation has been performed any party shall have liberty to apply for such further or other declaration or order as may be just.'

In practice, the purpose of the proceedings in relation to an adult patient will still be to establish whether or not the proposed sterilisation is in the best interests of the patient.

The proceedings will normally involve a thorough adversarial investigation of all possible viewpoints and any possible alternatives to sterilisation.

The role of the Official Solicitor and his investigation in these cases is helpfully set out in the Official Solicitor's Practice Note that has been referred to. The Practice Note also helpfully indicates to practitioners the particular evidence the court is likely to require on issues such as the patient's mental capacity, as well as her risk of pregnancy, alternative methods of contraception and potential psychological damage.

The plaintiff or applicant should normally be a parent or one of those responsible for the care of the patient or those intending to carry out the proposed operation.

The patient must always be a party and should normally be a defendant or respondent. In cases in which the patient is a defendant, the patient's guardian ad litem should normally be the Official Solicitor. In any case in which the Official Solicitor does not represent the patient, he should be a defendant. There will be, in every case, a hearing before a High Court judge fixed for directions on the first open date after the passage of eight weeks from the issue of the originating summons.

The case will normally be heard in Chambers. If it is heard in open court, the court will usually take steps to preserve the anonymity of the patient and the patient's family by making appropriate orders under the Contempt of Court Act 1981 (*Re G (Adult Patient: Publicity)* [1995] 2 FLR 528.

10.2   BONE MARROW TRANSPLANT

A question which has arisen and been considered by the court is the donation of bone marrow by a donor who is incapable of giving consent, where a significant benefit will flow to another person. What is distinct here (as opposed to, for example, proposed sterilisation operations) is that there is a third party who is intended to benefit from the proposed medical treatment on the patient. Notwithstanding such distinction, pursuant to *Re F (Mental Patient: Sterilisation)* [1990] 2 AC 1, the lawfulness of taking bone marrow from an adult donor who is incapable of giving consent will depend upon whether the treatment is in the best interests of the patient. The court will thereby have to be satisfied that the procedure envisaged will benefit the patient and, accordingly, benefits which may flow to the third party are relevant only insofar as they have a positive effect on the best interests of the patient.

It is helpful to scrutinise in this regard the case of *Re Y (Mental Incapacity: Bone Marrow Transplant)* [1996] 2 FLR 787. In that case, the patient was a severely mentally and physically handicapped young woman aged 25. Since birth, she suffered from hydrocephalus and required assistance in all her daily needs, except feeding. She was incapable of understanding what was said to her and understood her own basic needs only but not the needs of others. The plaintiff was the eldest of the patient's sisters and suffered from pre-leukaemic bone marrow disorder, myelodispastic syndrome. She urgently required a bone marrow transplant, preferably from sibling transplantation which, according to medical opinion, produced the best results for a significant prolongation of life. Although the patient had lived away from the family since the age of 10, first in a residential school and then in a community home, the family were closely knit and over the years had kept in touch with the patient, especially her mother who visited regularly and with whom the patient had the closest relationship. The mother also suffered from ill-health, had had a recent coronary by-pass operation and suffered from angina. Her condition was further exacerbated by her anxieties over the health of the sister. With the agreement of the family and the support of the

Official Solicitor, the guardian ad litem of the patient, the sister applied for a declaration that blood tests and a bone marrow harvesting operation under general anaesthetic could lawfully be performed upon the patient, despite the fact that she (the patient) was unable to give an informed consent for such procedures.

The appropriate test applied, as previously indicated, was whether the evidence showed that it was in the best interests of the patient for the procedures to take place. The findings of the court were as follows. The fact that the process would significantly benefit the sister was not relevant, unless, as a result of the patient helping her sister in that way, the best interests of the patient were served. The evidence showed that the patient benefited from the visits of her family and her occasional involvement in family events, since they maintained a link with the outside world which was helpful to her. Further, the patient showed an obvious affection with her mother which demonstrated that her mother held a special place in the patient's world. If the application was unsuccessful, the chances of the plaintiff sister not surviving were materially increased, which would have an adverse effect on her mother's health and the mother would be unable to maintain regular contact with the patient. In those circumstances, the defendant patient would clearly be harmed by the reduction in or loss of contact with her mother. Accordingly, the court held, it was to the benefit of the patient that she should act as a donor to her sister because her positive relationship with both her mother and sister would be prolonged and improved. Since the disadvantages to the patient were very small and no real long-term risk from a bone marrow harvesting would be caused, it was to the defendant's emotional, psychological and social benefit to grant the declaration sought.

There is, in this country, no express statutory provision governing incompetent adults or minors as bone marrow donors. Children frequently act as bone marrow donors. 'Bone marrow' falls outside the scope of the Human Organ Transplants Act 1989, which gives express permission to the use of live organ donations, under certain restricted circumstances. The European Bioethics Convention signed by a number of Member States but not, as yet, by this country, allows only regenerative tissue to be removed from minors and incompetent adults and in the following circumstances. The donation must have the potential to be life-saving. There must be no compatible competent adult donor. The recipient must be a brother or sister of the donor. The potential donor must not object to the proposed operation and written consent must be obtained on such a donor's behalf from a parent, legal representative or other competent authority: Council of Europe, Convention for the protection of human rights and dignity of the human beings with regard to the application of biology and medicine (adopted by the Committee of Ministers, 19 November 1996).

10.3   THE HUMAN FERTILISATION AND EMBRYOLOGY ACT 1990

Profound legal and ethical issues have arisen as to whether and how medical intervention should occur in the human reproductive process. One of the principal purposes in passing the 1990 Act was to set up a system of tight control within the UK of 'Treatment Services', defined in s 2(1) as 'Medical, Surgical or Obstetric Services provided to the public or a section of the public for the purpose of assisting women to carry children'. An authority independent of government, namely the Human Fertilisation and Embryology Authority (HFEA), was set up by the Act to exercise control. The principal mechanism of control is a compulsory system of licensing those who wish to provide treatment services, or to offer facilities for the storage of gametes (namely sperm and eggs), or to create, keep or use embryos for the purposes of research. The Act makes it a criminal offence to create, keep or use an embryo, except in pursuance of a licence. The power to grant and to revoke a licence is vested in committees set up by the Authority and they are obliged to inspect the premises where the proposed activities are to be conducted.

It is intended below to scrutinise three aspects only arising out of the Act.

10.3.1   The consent of donors to the use of their gametes

Generally, an effective consent in writing needs to be provided under Sch 3 to the Act, since a person's gametes must not be used (para 5) and must not be kept in storage (para 8) unless there is an effective consent by that person to their being so used or kept in storage. Nor can any person under s 4(1) and (2) of the Act store any gametes, or use the sperm of any man or use the eggs of any other woman, except through a licence.

However, under s 4(1)(b) and para 5(3) of Sch 3 to the Act, in certain circumstances only, the requirements of a licence for treatment and statutory consent under the Act are not necessary. The first circumstance is where the eggs are those of the patient herself and are being used for her purposes during her treatment. The second circumstance is where the sperm of a man is being used for the treatment together of a woman and that man. The meaning and interpretation of the notion of the provision or receipt of treatment services 'for or by a woman and a man together' was considered by the court in *Re B (Parentage)* [1996] 2 FLR 15. There, the mother applied pursuant to Sch 1 to the Children Act 1989 for financial provision for the children. As a preliminary point, the father raised the question of whether he was the parent of the children within the meaning of Sch 1 to the 1989 Act. The father had donated sperm, which was intended for the insemination of the mother, but, prior to insemination taking place, he had parted from the mother and at that stage his consent was not sought to the actual insemination. The question which arose for consideration by the judge was as to whether, in those circumstances, the mother and father were being treated together for the purposes of para 5(3) of Sch 3 to the 1990 Act. The father had given sperm as a part of a joint enterprise with the mother. He had attended hospital to give sperm not as an anonymous donor but playing his essential role in aiding the mother to achieve a pregnancy which was what both had been trying for. In those circumstances, the judge determined that the mother and father were receiving treatment services together. Consequently, the father was to be treated in law as the father of the children and, therefore, was a parent of the children within the terms of Sch 1 to the Children Act 1989.

In *R v Human Fertilisation and Embryology Authority, ex parte Blood* [1997] 2 WLR 806, the issue that arose was whether the patient could be treated with the sperm of her husband who had died. The facts were as follows. The applicant, Mrs Blood, was 27 years old when she married her husband in 1991. Towards the end of 1994, the couple actively began trying to start a family. The applicant had not conceived, when on 26 February 1995, her husband contracted meningitis. Two days later, he was in a coma. On 28 February 1995, Mrs Blood raised with the doctors the question of taking a sample of sperm by electro-ejaculation from her husband then, as indicated, in a coma. A sample was taken on 1 March 1995 and was entrusted to the Infertility Research Trust. A second sample was taken the following day, shortly before her husband was certified clinically dead. Both samples of sperm were kept by the Trust, pending the legal proceedings. The applicant wanted to use the samples to have her husband's child.

If Mr Blood had survived and the sperm had been immediately used as part of a course of treatment for himself and his wife while he was still alive, then the exception to the requirement of the licence for the treatment under s 4(1)(b) would have applied. Furthermore, as it would not have been necessary for the treatment to be 'in pursuance of a licence', there would have been no statutory requirement for the consent of Mr Blood to its use because the treatment would have been outside the statutory control.

As it was, the HFEA contended that the use and storage of his sperm under the Act was not permissible, since there was no written consent by him for those purposes in compliance with Sch 3 to the Act. Nor was the HFEA willing to permit the export of the sperm. In that context, the applicant submitted that the prohibition of the export of her late husband's sperm was an infringement of her freedom to receive cross-border services in other EU Member States. It was contended that, as a citizen of the UK, she had a directly enforceable right to medical treatment in another Member State under Articles 59 and 60 of the Treaty of Rome. It was held by the Court of Appeal that the HFEA had not taken into account sufficiently either the effect of Article 59 or the fact that, after its judgment, there should be no further cases where sperm was preserved without consent. The decision of the HFEA of 21 November 1996 was set aside and the HFEA was invited to reconsider the question of export of the sperm. In doing so, it would have to decide whether to allow or refuse it on grounds acceptable according to EC law. Such reconsideration occurred and Mrs Blood was permitted to receive treatment in Belgium. Her son was born in December 1998.

10.3.2   Maternity, paternity and non-genetic paternity

Maternity
Section 27 of the 1990 Act provides for maternity. By virtue of s 27(1) and (3), the woman who is carrying, or has carried, a child as a result of the placing in her of an embryo or of sperm and eggs, and no other woman, is to be treated as the mother of the child. Under UK law, this is the case, regardless of the law of the country in which the procedure occurred.

Non-genetic paternity
The Act of 1990 provides for and defines paternity where, in differing circumstances (dependent on whether the parties are married or unmarried), the creation of the embryo carried by the man's wife or partner was not brought about with his sperm.

Section 28(2) of the Act provides for non-genetic paternity in the case of some married men. So far as is material, it reads:

> 'If—
> (a)   at the time of the placing in her of the embryo or the sperm and eggs or of her insemination, the woman was a party to a marriage, and
> (b)   the creation of the embryo carried by her was not brought about with the sperm of the other party to the marriage,
> then ... the other party to the marriage shall be treated as the father of the child unless it is shown that he did not consent to the placing in her of the embryo or the sperm and eggs or to her insemination (as the case may be).'

Section 28(3) of the Act makes provision for non-genetic paternity in relation to the unmarried man:

> 'If no man is treated, by virtue of subsection (2) above, as the father of the child, but—
> (a)   the embryo ... was placed in the woman ... in the course of treatment services provided for her and a man together by a person to whom a licence applies, and
> (b)   the creation of the embryo carried by her was not brought about with the sperm of that man,
> then ... that man shall be treated as the father of the child.'

The distinction, accordingly, in this regard, as between the married man and the unmarried man is as follows. The married man is treated in law as the father unless it is shown that he did not consent to the placement within his wife. The unmarried man is treated in law as the father only if it is shown that the placement within the woman occurred in the course of treatment services provided for her and him together by a person to whom a licence applies.

In the case of *U v W (Attorney-General Intervening)* [1997] 2 FLR 282, the applicant mother of twin boys claimed that the respondent was the father by virtue of s 28 (3) of the 1990 Act. She was applying, pursuant to s 27 of the Child Support Act 1991, for declarations that the respondent was the father of the twins. The respondent, who was never married to the applicant, denied that he was the twins' father. The children were born by virtue of the placement into the uterus of the mother by a doctor in Rome of embryos fertilised by the conjunction of eggs taken from her with sperm provided, not by the respondent but by an anonymous donor. The respondent denied that he fell within s 28(3) of the 1990 Act on each of two grounds. The first ground was that the treatment services in the course of which the embryos were placed in the applicant were not 'provided for them together' but for the applicant mother alone. The second ground was that the doctor in Rome was not 'a person to whom a licence applied'. On the first ground, the doctor had told the couple that of the 12 of the applicant's eggs he had fertilised, one of them was with the respondent's sperm, while the others were with donor sperm. After the applicant had given birth to the twins, tests confirmed her genetic maternity but excluded the respondent from genetic paternity. The respondent conceded that, insofar as in the course of their relationship treatment services were provided with a view to the use of his own sperm in the fertilisation of the applicant's eggs, the services were provided for them together. However, the respondent argued that the embryos placed in the applicant were not embryos fertilised with his sperm. The objective of using his sperm, he contended, had been abandoned by the time when the embryos were placed in the applicant. The judge held, on the facts, that the doctor had placed the embryos in the applicant in the course of treatment services provided for her and the respondent together. However, the second ground of the respondent's case was upheld by the judge. He determined that as the treatment had not been administered by a licensed holder as it had taken place abroad, s 28(3) could not apply to confer paternity on the respondent. The judge further rejected the mother's contention that, in requiring treatment under licence, s 28(3) of the 1990 Act infringed Article 59 of the Treaty of Rome.

Genetic or 'biological' paternity
Section 28(4) of the Act provides that, where a person is treated as the father of the child by virtue of s 28(2) or (3), no other person is to be treated as the father of the child. Accordingly, the sperm donor is excluded from paternity whenever non-genetic paternity arises.

Section 28(6)(a) of the 1990 Act provides for exclusion of the sperm donor from paternity in certain circumstances, even when non-genetic paternity does not arise: the circumstances are, broadly, that the donor should have given a written and informed consent to the use of his sperm pursuant to Sch 3 to the Act.

There may be no question of non-genetic paternity arising and the donor of the sperm may not have given effective consent under the Act to the use of his sperm. Further, such sperm may not have been used for the treatment of the donor and the woman together. The question then arises as to the status of a child born as a result of artificial insemination by sperm from a donor who did not give an effective consent. The Act is silent on the question.

An act of sexual intercourse is not a prerequisite to fatherhood. Fatherhood concerns genetics and the provision of sperm which results in the birth of a child, unless either there is a presumption of legitimacy which affects the situation or there is statutory intervention, such as, for example, the change of status afforded by adoption or freeing for adoption: *Re B (Parentage)* [1996] 2 FLR 15 at 21. Subject to those matters, accordingly in common law such a donor would be the father of the child.

10.3.3   Parental orders relating to a child born to a surrogate mother

Such a parental order may only be made in favour of a married couple. The relevant statutory provision in this regard under the Act is set out as follows. By s 30:

> '(1) the court may make an order providing for a child to be treated in law as the child of the parties to the marriage (referred to in this section as "the husband" and "the wife") if—
> (a)   The child has been carried by a woman other than the wife as the result of the placing in her of an embryo or sperm and eggs or her artificial insemination,
> (b)   The gametes of the husband or the wife, or both, were used to bring about the creation of the embryo, and
> (c)   The conditions in subsections (2) to (7) below are satisfied.
> (2) The husband and the wife must apply for an order within six months of the birth of the child ...
> (3) At the time of the application and of the making of the order—
> (a)   the child's home must be with the husband and the wife, and
> (b)   the husband or the wife, or both of them, must be domiciled in a part of the United Kingdom ...
> (4) At the time of the making of the order both the husband and the wife must have attained the age of eighteen.
> (5) The court must be satisfied that both the father of the child (including a person who is the father by virtue of section 28 of this Act), where he is not the husband, and the woman who carried the child have freely, and with full understanding of what is involved, agreed unconditionally to the making of the order.
> (6) Subsection (5) does not require the agreement of the person who cannot be found or is incapable of giving agreement and the agreement of the woman who carried the child is ineffective for the purposes of that subsection if given by her less than six weeks after the child's birth.
> (7) The court must be satisfied that no money or other benefit (other than for expenses reasonably incurred) has been given or received by the husband or the wife for or in consideration of—
> (a)   the making of the order,
> (b)   any agreement required by subsection (5) above,
> (c)   the handing over of the child to the husband and the wife, or
> (d)   the making of any arrangements with a view to the making of the order,
> unless authorised by the court.'

10.4 BLOOD TESTS

Section 20(1) of the Family Law Reform Act 1969 states as follows:

> 'In any civil proceedings in which the paternity of any person falls to be determined by the Court hearing the proceedings, the Court may on an application by any party to the proceedings, give a direction for the use of blood tests to ascertain whether such tests show that a party to the proceedings is or is not thereby excluded from being the father of that person . . .'

It is clear under the inherent jurisdiction, as decided by the House of Lords in *S (An Infant, by her guardian ad litem the Official Solicitor to the Supreme Court) v S; W v Official Solicitor (acting as guardian ad litem for a male infant named PHW)* [1972] AC 24, and also under s 21(1) of the Family Law Reform Act 1969, that an adult cannot be forced to provide a blood sample against his or her will.

However, s 23(1) of the Act provides that, where a court gives a direction under s 20 and any person fails to take any step required of him for the purposes of giving effect to the direction, the court may draw such inferences, if any, from that fact as appears proper in the circumstances.

Section 20(1) of the Act does not empower the court to order blood tests, but merely permits it to make a direction for the use of blood tests to ascertain paternity (*In Re H (A Minor)* [1997] Fam 89).

Whereas the welfare of the child is the paramount consideration in deciding, for example, an application for parental responsibility and contact in an application under s 20 of the 1969 Act, the paramountcy test does not apply. The child's welfare is an important factor to be weighed alongside a number of other factors, including, for example, whether there is a refusal of a party to undergo blood testing and the likely outcome of the proceedings in which the issue arises. Nevertheless, the court should refuse to make a direction for the use of a blood test to ascertain paternity, if satisfied that it would be against the child's interests to order it (*In Re H (A Minor)* [1997] Fam 89 at 103, 104).

Section 21(3) of the 1969 Act states that:

> 'a blood sample may be taken from a person under the age of sixteen years . . . if the person who has the care and control of him consents.'

In the case of *In Re R (A Minor) (Blood Tests: Constraint)* [1998] Fam 66, an issue of paternity arose in respect of a child aged 22 months. The court was satisfied that it was in the child's best interests that her paternity should be determined, if at all possible, but the mother was not prepared to give her consent under s 21(3) of the Family Law Reform Act 1969 to blood samples being taken. The question then arose as to whether and how the blood tests could be effected. The court held that there was nothing in principle to prevent the court, under its inherent jurisdiction, from requiring a child under 16 to provide a blood sample, if satisfied that that was the right course. Nevertheless, on the facts, it was held to be possible to implement the terms of s 21(3) by making a direction under s 20 for the provision of a blood sample and ordering the delivery of the child for that specific purpose into the care and control of the Official Solicitor, granting him permission to consent on the child's behalf.

10.5   EUTHANASIA

'Euthanasia' connotes the receipt of medical help to actively cause the death of a patient to avoid or to end his or her suffering. It is espoused by the Voluntary Euthanasia Society whose aim is to make it legal for a competent adult, who is suffering severe distress from an incurable illness, to receive medical help to die at his or her considered and persistent request.

Euthanasia is not lawful at common law. The Report of the House of Lords Select Committee on Medical Ethics was published in January 1994 and rejected any suggestion of the legalisation of voluntary euthanasia. It further rejected the creation of a new offence of 'mercy-killing'. The Government has indicated no intention of proposing legislation on euthanasia to Parliament. Such is clear from the Government's Consultation Paper entitled 'Who Decides?'.

The English criminal law draws a sharp distinction between acts and omissions. If an act resulting in death is done without lawful excuse and with intent to kill, it is murder. But an omission to act with the same result and with the same intent is, in general, no offence at all. There is one important general exception at common law, namely that a person may be criminally liable for the consequences of an omission if he stands in such a relation to the victim that he is under a duty to act.

It is helpful here to indicate a lengthy passage from the judgment of Lord Goff in *Airedale NHS Trust v Bland* [1993] AC 789 at 865:

> 'I must however stress, at this point, that the law draws a crucial distinction between cases in which a doctor decides not to provide, or to continue to provide, for his patient treatment or care which could or might prolong his life, and those in which he decides, for example by administering a lethal drug, actively to bring his patient's life to an end. As I have already indicated, the former may be lawful, either because the doctor is giving effect to his patient's wishes by withholding the treatment or care, or even in certain circumstances in which ... the patient is incapacitated from stating whether or not he gives his consent. But it is not lawful for a doctor to administer a drug to his patient to bring about his death, even though that course is prompted by a humanitarian desire to end his suffering, however great that suffering may be: see *R v Cox* (unreported) 18 September 1992. So to act is to cross the Rubicon which runs between on the one hand the care of the living patient and on the other hand euthanasia – actively causing his death to avoid or to end his suffering. Euthanasia is not lawful at common law. It is of course well known that there are many responsible members of our society who believe that euthanasia should be made lawful; but that result could, I believe, only be achieved by legislation which expresses the democratic will that so fundamental a change should be made in our law, and can, if enacted, ensure that such legalised killing can only be carried out subject to appropriate supervision and control. It is true that the drawing of this distinction may lead to a charge of hypocrisy; because it can be asked why, if the doctor, by

discontinuing treatment, is entitled in consequence to let his patient die, it should not be lawful to put him out of his misery straight away, in a more humane manner, by a lethal injection, rather than let him linger on in pain until he dies. But the law does not feel able to authorise euthanasia, even in circumstances such as these; for once euthanasia is recognised as lawful in these circumstances, it is difficult to see any logical basis for excluding it in others.'

It is an established rule that a doctor may, when caring for a patient who is, for example, dying of cancer, lawfully administer pain-killing drugs despite the fact that he knows that an incidental effect of that application will be to abbreviate the patient's life. Such a decision may properly be made as part of the care of the living patient, in his best interests and, on this basis, the treatment will be lawful. Moreover, where the doctor's treatment of his patient is lawful, the patient's death will be regarded in law as exclusively caused by the injury or disease to which his condition is attributable: per Lord Goff in *Airedale NHS Trust v Bland* [1993] AC 789 at 867.

Many believe, commensurate with the sanctity of life, that euthanasia is wrong as a matter of principle. They take the view that a person should live until life ends naturally, regardless of the pain he or she has to endure, although they may accept that a doctor may use pain-killers to relieve pain, even where these may have the incidental effect of shortening life.

A report on euthanasia by a Working Party of the British Medical Association published in 1988 concluded that the current distinction between an act and omission to act was legitimate and should be maintained. Among the reasons given for reaching this conclusion were the following.

(i)   Experience, for instance at hospices, suggests that euthanasia requests often represent something other than a request to be killed. They may often be a veiled enquiry whether people can be bothered about the patient anymore.
(ii) A decision to terminate life allows no respite for re-evaluation and may well not be fully informed. Very few people who have been saved from a serious suicide attempt make another attempt to kill themselves.
(iii) Patients will often acquiesce in treatment simply because the necessary arrangements have been made. For the elderly and lonely, in particular, the courage required to back out of a process once it has started may be too much for them.

10.5.1   Criminality and 'mercy-killing'

The fact that a doctor's motives are kindly may for some transform the moral quality of his act, but this makes no difference in law. It is intent to kill or cause grievous bodily harm which constitutes the mens rea of murder, and the reason why the intent was formed makes no difference at all. Further, there is no difference in law if the patient consents to, or indeed urges, the ending of his life by active means. In 'consenting' to being killed, the interests of the State in preserving life override the otherwise all-powerful interest of the patient's autonomy. The case of *R v Cox* [1992] 12 BMLR 38 illustrates these points. Dr Cox was a consultant rheumatologist at a hospital in the South of England. Among his patients was a lady who had long suffered from arthritis. Between 1973 and her death in 1991 she had been admitted to the hospital no fewer than 21 times. Dr Cox was the consultant in charge of her case from the date of his appointment in 1978 until the day she died. She suffered terrible pain from her affliction. She was treated with pain-killers in increasing quantities. Merely touching her body caused her intense pain and there were times when she was said to have howled like a dog in her agony. In the last few days before she died, she was begging the doctors to kill her. Dr Cox was clearly distressed by her suffering and, in the end, he gave her an injection of potassium chloride. The patient died very shortly afterwards. Dr Cox administered the injection without any attempt at concealment in the presence of a nurse and his registrar. He thereafter recorded what he had done in the relevant records. He was charged and brought to trial before a judge and jury. The charge was not murder but attempted murder on the basis that, since the patient was so close to death when she received the injection, it was impossible to be sure that it was the injection which caused her death, rather than natural causes. The distinction between the two possible charges was that, in relation to a conviction for murder, there would inevitably be a life sentence of imprisonment but in relation to attempted murder sentencing upon conviction would be in the discretion of the judge. Dr Cox was convicted of attempted murder but he was sentenced to one year's imprisonment, which was suspended. The judge, whilst accepting that the doctor had acted only from motives of mercy, nevertheless reprimanded the doctor for having departed from established standards of medical ethics when he gave his patient the lethal injection. In subsequent disciplinary proceedings before the Professional Conduct Committee of the General Medical Council, he was not struck off the register nor even suspended from practice. He was simply admonished.

10.6 SUICIDE

Section 2 of the Suicide Act 1961 makes it an offence to aid, abet, counsel or procure another to commit suicide, or attempt to do so, although suicide itself is no longer a crime. Under s 4(1) of the Homicide Act 1957:

> 'It shall be manslaughter and shall not be murder for a person acting in pursuance of a suicide pact between him and another to kill the other or be a party to the other ... being killed by a third person.'

10.7 ABORTION

A child capable of being born alive is protected by the criminal law from intentional destruction, and, by the Abortion Act 1967, from termination otherwise than as permitted by the Act.

The Infant (Life Preservation) Act 1929, by s 1, provides a criminal offence for the intentional destruction of a child, capable of being born alive, before it has an existence independent of its mother.

Under the Abortion Act 1967, s 1 (as amended by the Human Fertilisation and Embryology Act 1990) pregnancies up to 24 weeks may in certain defined circumstances, be terminated. Pregnancies after 24 weeks may be terminated where it is necessary to prevent grave injury to the mental or physical health of the pregnant woman. The Act gives precedence to the health of the mother over the unborn child.

The position in law generally of the unborn child is examined in detail in Chapter 8 in relation to medical treatment as it pertains to minors. Applications seeking to prevent abortions taking place are also considered in Chapter 8 of this book.

10.8   THE REMOVAL OF BODY PARTS FOLLOWING DEATH

Tissues removed from a patient for diagnostic purposes during the currency of his life remain the property of that patient and must be returned to the patient if he wishes. However, it is the present state of the law that there is no property in a dead body: *Williams v Williams* (1882) 20 ChD 659 at 662–663. There are two circumstances here to consider. The first is where the person lawfully in possession of the body of a deceased person may authorise the removal of any part of it under the Human Tissue Act 1961. This may emanate from a person's request under s 1(1) of the Act that his body, or any specified part, be used after his death for therapeutic purposes or for purposes of medical education or research. Such a request, in practice, will be implemented only if the next of kin do not object to such use. Alternately, the person lawfully in possession of the body of a deceased person may, under s 1(2) of the Act and for the above-mentioned purposes, authorise the removal of any part from the body:

> 'If, having made such reasonable enquiry as may be practicable, he has no reason to believe:
>
> (a)   that the deceased had expressed an objection to his body being so dealt with after his death, and had not withdrawn it; and
> (b)   that the surviving spouse or any surviving relative of the deceased objects to the body being so dealt with.'

The second circumstance arises from the removal of body parts during a post-mortem examination and their subsequent retention or disposal. Where the post-mortem examination is requested or directed by the coroner, by r 9 of the Coroners Rules 1984, SI 1984/552, a doctor will be under an obligation to make provision for the preservation of body material which, in his opinion, bears upon the cause of death, but only for such period as the coroner thinks fit. A post-mortem examination (other than one directed or requested by a coroner) will only occur with the consent of the next of kin of the deceased, who are invited to sign a consent form. Doctors may wish to retain tissues or organs removed from a body during an autopsy for further diagnostic purposes or for medical education or research. Concern has arisen that next of kin of the deceased may not know whether any parts of the body have been removed or what particular parts have been removed. They may also then be unaware that any such parts have been subsequently either retained or disposed of. The uncertainty, from the next of kin's point of view, may arise from a consent form which includes wording merely to the effect that tissues may be kept for diagnostic purposes or for medical education or research. Other consent forms may be more explicit, specifying, for example, that the whole brain, or heart, or both, may be retained. The next of kin are then able to consider a full or limited consent to the proposed autopsy, or a refusal of consent to such autopsy occurring. The difficulties in law as to who, if anyone, may be said to own, possess or control, at varying times, any such removed body parts are reflected in the case of *Dobson and Another v North Tyneside Health Authority and Another* [1997] 1 FLR 598. The Court of Appeal held that the health authority had been entitled to dispose of the brain which had been removed during the autopsy, once the cause of death had been determined by the coroner and the time for challenge to that determination had passed. In other circumstances where a body part or parts have been retained without the knowledge of the next of kin and they then become aware of such retention, discussion will ensue as to what the next of kin wish should be done with the part or parts. Guidelines are to be forthcoming in the near future from the Royal College of Pathology and the Coroners Society. Whether, and to what extent, a broader review of the law in this area is to take place remains to be seen. Such a review certainly appears long overdue.

Part III

APPENDED MATERIALS

CONTENTS

1   Criteria for the diagnosis of brain stem death

REVIEW BY A WORKING GROUP CONVENED BY THE ROYAL COLLEGE OF PHYSICIANS AND ENDORSED BY THE CONFERENCE OF MEDICAL ROYAL COLLEGES AND THEIR FACULTIES IN THE UNITED KINGDOM

This review of the criteria used in the diagnosis of brain stem death (hitherto known as brain death) has been produced to update earlier documents on this subject published by the Conference of Medical Royal Colleges and their Faculties (Conference of Colleges) between 1976 and 1981[1-4] and the relevant sections of the Department of Health revised guidelines published in 1983.[5]

The definition of death

It is suggested that 'irreversible loss of the capacity for consciousness, combined with irreversible loss of the capacity to breathe' should be regarded as the definition of death. The irreversible cessation of brain stem function (brain stem death) whether induced by intracranial events or the result of extracranial phenomena such as anoxia will produce the forementioned clinical state and therefore brain stem death is equivalent to the death of the individual. It is suggested that the more correct term 'brain stem death' should henceforth replace the term 'brain death' used in previous papers produced by the Conference of Colleges and the Department of Health.

The diagnosis of brain stem death

The clinical criteria for the diagnosis of brain stem death identified by the Conference of Colleges during the period 1976–1981 have been confirmed by all published series and have therefore been adequately validated.

(a)   *The beating heart in brain stem death.* Even if ventilation is continued, both adults and children will suffer cessation of heart beat within a few days, very occasionally a few weeks, of the diagnosis of brain stem death.

(b)   *Endocrinological and metabolic abnormalities.* Endocrinological abnormalities, such as diabetes insipidus, biochemical abnormalities, such as hypo- or hypernatraemia, and hypothermia may occur in patients following anoxic, haemorrhagic or traumatic cerebral injury. These endocrinological abnormalities may be consequences of brain stem failure and must be differentiated from causative abnormalities of endocrinological, biochemical or autonomic function.

(c)   *Limb and trunk movements.* Reflex movements of the limbs and torso may occur after brain stem death. The doctor should be able to explain clearly the significance of these movements to relatives, who should understand that they are of a reflex and not a voluntary nature.

(d) *Investigtions.* The accuracy of the clinical criteria for the diagnosis of brian stem death during the past 17 years provides justification for not including the results of neurophysiological or imaging investigations as part of those criteria. At present there is no evidence that imaging, electroencephalography or evoked potentials assist in the determination of brain stem death and, though such techniques will be kept under review, they should not presently form part of the diagnostic requirements.

(e) *Children and the very young.* A report of a working party of the British Paediatric Association in 1991,[6] supported by the Council of the Royal College of Physicians suggested that, in children over the age of two months, the brain stem death criteria should be the same as those in adults. There is insufficient information on children under the age of two months and on premature babies to define guidelines. A working party of the Conference of Colleges on *Organ transplantation in neonates* in 1988[7] recommended that organs for transplantation may be removed from anencephalic infants when two doctors who are not members of the transplant team agree that spontaneous respiration has ceased.

(f) *The persistent vegetative state.* Problems relating to the diagnosis and management of the persistent vegetative state must not be confused with those relating to brain stem death.

(g) *Peripheral neurological syndromes of critical care.* There is a range of overlapping neuropathic, neuromuscular and myopathic syndromes which may occur in the context of critical care and may cause problems in weaning a patient from a ventilator. This is not true apnoea (respiratory centre paralysis) and should not be taken as evidence of brain stem death.

CONDITIONS UNDER WHICH THE DIAGNOSIS OF BRAIN STEM DEATH SHOULD BE CONSIDERED

(1) There should be no doubt that the patient's condition is due to irremediable brain damage of known aetiology (see Note 1).

(2) The patient is deeply comatose
   (a) There should be no suspicion that this state is due to depressant drugs (see Note 2);
   (b) Primary hypothermia as a cause of coma must have been excluded;
   (c) Potentially reversible metabolic and endocrine disturbances must have been excluded as the likely cause of the continuation of coma. It is recognised that metabolic and endocrine disturbances are a likely accompaniment of brain stem death (eg hyponatraemia, diabetes insipidus) but these are the effect rather than the cause of that condition and do not preclude the diagnosis of brain stem death.

(3) The patient is being maintained on the ventilator because spontaneous respiration has become inadequate or ceased altogether (see Note 3).

It is essential that these conditions be satisfied before the diagnosis of brain stem death is considered or further investigated.

Notes:

1 It may be obvious within hours of a primary intracranial event such as severe head injury, spontaneous intracranial haemorrhage or following neurosurgery that the condition is irremediable. However, when a patient has suffered primarily from cardiac arrest, hypoxia or severe circulatory insufficiency with an indefinite period of cerebral anoxia, or is suspected of having cerebral air or fat embolism, it may take longer to establish the diagnosis and to be confident of the prognosis. In some patients the primary pathology may be a matter of doubt and a confident diagnosis may only be reached by continuity of clinical observation and investigation.

2 Narcotics, hypnotics and tranquillisers may have prolonged duration of action, particularly when hypothermia co-exists or in the context of renal or hepatic failure. The benzodiazepines are markedly cumulative and persistent in their actions and are commonly used as anti-convulsants or to assist synchronisation with mechanical ventilators. It is therefore essential that the drug history should be carefully reviewed and any possibility of intoxication being the cause of or contributing to the patient's comatose state should preclude a diagnosis of brain stem death. It is important to recognise that in some patients anoxia may have followed the ingestion of a drug but in this situation the criteria for brain stem death will not be applicable until such time as the drug effects have been excluded.

3 Relaxants (neuromuscular blocking agents) and other drugs must have been excluded as the cause of respiratory inadequacy or failure. Immobility, unresponsiveness, and lack of spontaneous respiration may be due to the use of neuromuscular blocking drugs and the persistence of their effects should be excluded by the elicitation of deep tendon reflexes or by the demonstration of adequate neuromuscular conduction with a conventional nerve stimulator. Persistent effects of hypnotics or narcotics must be excluded as the cause of respiratory failure.

References

1   Conference of Medical Royal Colleges and their Faculties in the United Kingdom. Diagnosis of brain death. *Br Med J* 1976;**ii**: 1187–8.
2   Conference of Medical Royal Colleges and their Faculties in the United Kingdom. Diagnosis of brain death. *Lancet* 1976;**ii**: 1069–70.
3   Conference of Medical Royal Colleges and their Faculties in the United Kingdom. Diagnosis of death. *Br Med J* 1979;**i**: 332.
4   Conference of Medical Royal Colleges and their Faculties in the United Kingdom. Diagnosis of death. *Lancet* 1979;**i**: 261–2.
5   Health Departments of Great Britain and Northern Ireland. *Cadaveric organs for transplantation: a code of practice including the diagnosis of brain death.* London: HMSO, 1983.
6   British Paediatric Association. *Diagnosis of brain stem death in infants and children.* Report of a working party. London: BPA, 1991.
7   Conference of Medical Royal Colleges and their Faculties in the United Kingdom. *Organ transplantation in neonates.* London: Royal College of Physicians, 1988.

Members of the working group

Sir Douglas Black (Chairman); **Professor Sir Leslie Turnberg** President, Royal College of Physicians; **Professor David London** Registrar, Royal College of Physicians; **Dr D Bates** Consultant Neurologist, Royal Victoria Infirmary, Newcastle upon Tyne; **Dr N Melia** Observer, Department of Health; **Dr C Pallis** Reader Emeritus in Neurology, Royal Postgraduate Medical School, Hammersmith; **Dr P F Prior** formerly Consultant in charge of Clinical Neurophysiology, St Bartholomew's Hospital, London; **Mr K Rolles** Consultant Surgeon and Director of the Liver Transplant Unit, The Royal Free Hospital, London (representing the Royal College of Surgeons); **Dr J C Stoddart** formerly

Consultant Anaesthetist, Royal Victoria Infirmary, Newcastle upon Tyne (representing the Royal College of Anaesthetists); **Dr C R Kennedy** Consultant Paediatric Neurologist, Southampton General Hospital; **Professor J D Pickard** Bayer Professor of Neurosurgery, University of Cambridge.

Source: *Journal of the Royal College of Physicians of London* Vol 29 No 5 September/ October 1995.

2   The permanent vegetative state

REVIEW BY A WORKING GROUP CONVENED BY THE ROYAL COLLEGE OF PHYSICIANS AND ENDORSED BY THE CONFERENCE OF MEDICAL ROYAL COLLEGES AND THEIR FACULTIES OF THE UNITED KINGDOM

The working group was convened following a recommendation of the House of Lords Select Committee on Medical Ethics that PVS should be defined and a code of practice developed relating to its management.[1]

Defining the vegetative state

The Working Group recognises that the commonly used acronymn 'PVS' can denote either the '*persistent* vegetative state'[2] or the '*permanent* vegetative state' and could thus lead to confusion. It is therefore recommended that the following terms and definitions should be used:

The vegetative state
A clinical condition of unawareness of self and environment in which the patient breathes spontaneously, has a stable circulation and shows cycles of eye closure and eye opening which may simulate sleep and waking. This may be a transient stage in the recovery from coma or it may persist until death.

The continuing vegetative state (CVS)
When the vegetative state continues for more than four weeks it becomes increasingly unlikely that the condition is part of a recovery phase from coma and the diagnosis of a continuing vegetative state can be made.

The permanent vegetative state (PVS)
A patient in a continuing vegetative state will enter a permanent vegetative state when the diagnosis of irreversibility can be established with a high degree of clinical certainty. It is a diagnosis which is not absolute but based on probabilities. Nevertheless, it may reasonably be made when a patient has been in a continuing vegetative state following head injury for more than 12 months or following other causes of brain damage for more than six months.[3,4] The diagnosis can be made at birth only in infants with anencephaly or hydranencephaly. For children with other severe malformations or acquired brain damage, observation for at least six months is recommended until lack of awareness can be established.

Criteria for diagnosis of permanent vegetative state

Preconditions

–   There shall be an established cause for the condition. It may be due to acute cerebral injury, degenerative conditions, metabolic disorders or developmental malformations.

- The persisting effects of sedative, anaesthetic or neuromuscular blocking drugs shall be excluded. It is recognised that drugs may have been the original cause of an acute cerebral injury, usually hypoxic, but their continuing direct effect must be excluded either by passage of time or by appropriate analysis of body fluids.
- Reversible metabolic causes shall be corrected or excluded as the cause. Metabolic disturbance may occur during the course of a vegetative state and are an inevitable consequence of the terminal stage but should have been ruled out as causative.

Clinical criteria

(1) There shall be no evidence of awareness of self or environment at any time. There shall be no volitional response to visual, auditory, tactile or noxious stimuli. There shall be no evidence of language comprehension or expression.
(2) There shall be the presence of cycles of eye closure and eye opening which may simulate sleep and waking.
(3) There shall be sufficiently preserved hypothalamic and brain stem function to ensure the maintenance of respiration and circulation.

These **three** clinical requirements shall **all** be fulfilled for the diagnosis to be considered.

Other clinical features are:

- There will be incontinence of bladder and bowel, spontaneous blinking and usually retained pupillary responses and corneal responses. The response to ice water caloric testing will be a tonic eye movement which can be conjugate or dysconjugate.
- There will not be nystagmus in response to ice water caloric testing, the patient will not have visual fixation, be able to track moving objects with the eyes or show a 'menace' response.
- There may be occasional movements of the head and eyes towards a peripheral sound or movement and there may be movement of the trunk and limbs in a purposeless way; some patients may appear to smile and the eyes may water, there may be a 'grimace' to painful stimuli. There may be startle myoclonus. These motor activities shall be inconsistent, non-purposeful and explicable as a reflex response to external stimuli. Deep tendon reflexes may be present and reduced, normal or brisk; plantar responses may be flexor or extensor; there may be clonus and other signs of spasticity. There may be roving eye movements.

Differential diagnosis (Table 1)
It is essential to distinguish the vegetative state from brain stem death, coma and the locked-in syndrome. The differentiation of these conditions is on clinical grounds; there is no evidence at present that electroencephalography, evoked potentials, computed tomography (CT) of the cranium or magnetic resonance imaging (MRI) of the cerebrum improve upon the clinical diagnosis. Patients who are in a permanent vegetative state may show changes of cortical atrophy and hydrocephalus on CT head scan, and positron emission tomography (PET) will show a reduction in cerebral metabolism; but neither finding is diagnostic of the permanent vegetative state.

The time course
There is evidence that the factors which influence the prognosis of patients in a continuing vegetative state are the cause of the condition and the length of time for which it has continued. In patients who are in a continuing vegetative state following causes other than

head injury there is very little hope of recovery of sentience after three months and none after six months. In patients who are in a continuing vegetative state after head injury the chances of recovery after six months are extremely low and, after 12 months non-existent.[3, 4] It is suggested that, whenever head injury is present, even when there is additional severe trauma, the longer of these time intervals be taken before the continuing vegetative state is termed 'permanent'.

Thus, the diagnosis of the permanent vegetative state should not be made before six months following non-head injury brain damage or 12 months following head injury.

The management of the patient in a vegetative state

Medical care
Prior to the diagnosis of a permanent vegetative state it is imperative that patients have a high quality of care with appropriate nursing or home care and that oxygenation, circulation and nutrition are maintained and complicating factors such as hypoglycaemia and infection corrected. Until there is firm scientific evidence that treatment, in terms of specific medical, physiotherapeutic or rehabilitative activities improves the outcome of patients in a continuing vegetative state it is a matter of clinical judgement as to the most appropriate measures, their application and the length of time they should be pursued. The medical staff must advise the relatives and carers of the situation during the continuing vegetative state.

Examination
When the diagnosis of a permanent vegetative state is being considered it is obligatory that the patient should be examined by two medical practitioners experienced in assessing disturbances of consciousness. They should undertake their own assessment separately and should write clearly the details of that assessment and their conclusion in the notes. They must ask medical and other clinical staff and relatives or carers about the reactions and responses of the patient and it is important that the assessors shall take into account the descriptions and comments given by relatives, carers and nursing staff who spend most time with the patient. The medical practitioners shall separately perform a formal neurological examination and consider the results of those investigations which have been undertaken to identify the cause of the condition. It is helpful for nursing staff and relatives to be present during the examination; their role as responsible witnesses who spend a much longer time with the patient than can the medical practitioners must be recognised.

Re-assessment
It is to be emphasised that there is no urgency in making the diagnosis of the permanent vegetative state. If there is any uncertainty in the mind of the assessor then the diagnosis shall not be made and a reassessment undertaken after further time has elapsed. The most important role of the medical practitioner in making the diagnosis is to ensure that the patient is not sentient and, in this respect, the views of nursing staff, relatives and carers are of considerable importance and help.

Final definitive diagnosis and decisions concerning life support
When the diagnosis of a permanent vegetative state has been established by (a) identification of the cause for the syndrome; (b) the clinical state of the patient; and (c) the lapse of time, recovery cannot be achieved and further therapy is futile. It merely prolongs an insentient life for the patient and a hopeless vigil for relatives and carers. The clinical

team of doctors and nurses, augmented when necessary by colleagues, should formally review the clinical evidence. The decision, when made on full evidence that the situation is, in lay terms, 'hopeless' should be communicated sensitively to the relatives who are then given time to consider the implications, including the possibility of withdrawing artificial means of administering food and fluid.[5, 6, 7] At present the courts require, as a matter of practice, that the decision to withdraw nutrition and hydration, resulting in the inevitable death of the patient, should be referred to the court before any action is taken.[8] A decision to withdraw other life sustaining medication such as insulin for diabetes may also need to be referred to the courts because the legal position on this is uncertain. By contrast, decisions not to intervene with cardio-pulmonary resuscitation or to prescribe antibiotics, dialysis and insulin are clinical decisions. Further, those responsible for the patient's care must take account of, and respect, the patient's own views when known, whether these are formally recorded in a written document (or advance directive) or not.[9] When the medical team is agreed on the course to be taken the relatives should be counselled and their views sought, but (subject to court involvement) the decision is for those professionals who have the responsibility for the care of the patient.

References

1   House of Lords. *Report of the Select Committee on Medical Ethics.* Session 1993–4. London: HMSO, 1994, (HL Paper 21-I).
2   Jennett B, Plum F. Persistent vegetative state after brain damage: a syndrome in search of a name. *Lancet* 1972;**1**:734–7.
3   Multi-Society Task Force on PVS. Medical aspects of the persistent vegetative state (first part). *N Engl J Med* 1994;**330**:1499–1508.
4   Multi-Society Task Force on PVS. Medical aspects of the persistent vegetative state (second part). *N Eng J Med* 1994;**330**:1572–9.
5   BMA Medical Ethics Committee. *Discussion paper on treatment of patients in persistent vegetative state.* London: BMA, 1992.
6   Institute of Medical Ethics Working Party on the Ethics of Prolonging Life and Assisting Death. Withdrawal of life-support from patients in a persistent vegetative state. *Lancet* 1993;**337**:96–8.
7   BMA Medical Ethics Committee. *BMA guidelines on treatment decisions of patients in a persistent vegetative state.* London: BMA, 1994.
8   Howard RS, Miller DH. The persistent vegetative state: information on prognosis allows decisions to be made on management. *Br Med J* 1995;**310**:341–2.
9   Doyal L. Advanced directives: like a will, everybody should have one. *Br Med J* 1995;**310**:612–13.

Table 1. Differentiation of vegetative state from other conditions

Condition	Vegetative state	Coma	Brain stem death	Locked-in syndrome
Self-awareness	Absent	Absent	Absent	Present
Cyclical eye opening	Present	Absent	Absent	Present
*Glasgow coma scale	A4,B1–4,C1	A1–2,B1–4,C1–2	A1,B1–2,C1	A4,B1,C1
Motor function	No purposeful movement	No purposeful movement	None or only reflex spinal movement	Eye movement preserved in the vertical plane and able to blink volitionally
Experience of pain	No	No	No	Yes
Respiratory function	Normal	Depressed or varied	Absent	Normal
EEG activity	Polymorphic delta or theta – sometimes slow alpha	Polymorphic delta or theta	Electrocerebral silence or theta	Normal or minimally abnormal
Cerebral metabolism	Reduced by 50% or more	Reduced by 50% or more	Absent or greatly reduced	Minimally or moderately reduced
Prognosis	Depends on cause and length	Recovery, vegetative state, or death within 2–4 weeks	No recovery	Depends on cause though recovery unlikely

*Glasgow Coma Scale:

A	Eye opening	B	Motor function	C	Verbal
1	No response	1	No response	1	None
2	To pain	2	Extension	2	Grunts
3	To voice	3	Flexion	3	Inappropriate words
4	Spontaneously	4	Flexion	4	Confused

Members of the working group

Sir Douglas Black (Chairman); **Professor D London** Registrar, Royal College of Physicians; **Dr D Bates** Consultant Neurologist, Royal Victoria Infirmary, Newcastle Upon Tyne; **Revd Professor G R Dunstan** member of Royal College of Physicians Committee on Ethics; **Dr K W M Fulford** Consultant Psychiatrist, Warneford Hospital, Oxford; **Dr E Gadd** Observer, Department of Health; **Mrs J Gaffin** Executive Director, National Council for Hospice and Specialist Palliative Care Services; **Professor A Grubb** Professor of Health Care Law, King's College, London; **Dr J S Horner** Chairman, Medical Ethics Committee, British Medical Association; **Rabbi Julia Neuberger** Chairman, Camden & Islington Community Health Services; **Professor J D Pickard** Bayer Professor of Neurosurgery, University of Cambridge; **Professor R O Robinson** Professor of Paediatric Neurology, Guy's Hospital; **Dr D L Stevens** Consultant Neurologist, Gloucestershire Royal Hospital.

Source: *Journal of the Royal College of Physicians of London* Vol 30 No 2 March/April 1996.

ADDENDUM TO A REVIEW BY A WORKING GROUP CONVENED BY THE ROYAL COLLEGE OF PHYSICIANS AND ENDORSED BY THE CONFERENCE OF MEDICAL ROYAL COLLEGES[1]

In 1994 The House of Lords Select Committee on Medical Ethics recommended that permanent vegetative state (PVS) should be defined and a code of practice developed relating to its management.[1] The Royal College of Physicians of London convened a working party which reported in 1996.[2] Shortly after this report was published an article appeared in the *British Medical Journal* suggesting that PVS was not infrequently misdiagnosed.[3] The working party met Dr Keith Andrews, the principal author of this paper to discuss whether the working party's recommendations should be altered in the light of his findings.

The working party concluded that further emphasis should be given to the following points in its report:

1. **'Re-assessment:** It is to be emphasised that there is no urgency in making the diagnosis of PVS. If there is any uncertainty in the mind of the assessor then the diagnosis shall not be made and a re-assessment undertaken after a further time has elapsed.'
2. **'Examination:** ... It is important that the assessors shall take into account the descriptions and accounts given by relatives, carers and nursing staff who spend most time with the patient.'

The examining physician will rarely have sufficient time to monitor the patient carefully throughout the day, so information from the para-medical staff, carers and family is of great importance in assessing the potential responsiveness of the patient. Since it has been suggested that the patient's position may affect responsiveness, patients should be assessed in different positions and should be managed in an environment that is stimulating, comforting and most suitable for their needs.

Apart from emphasising and fleshing out these points, the Working Party saw no reason to modify its report.[1]

References

1   House of Lords, *Report of the Select Committee on Medical Ethics*. Session 1993–4. London, HMSO, 1994 (HL Paper 21–1).
2   The permanent vegetative state. Report by a working group convened by the Royal College of Physicians and endorsed by the Conference of Medical Royal Colleges and their Faculties of the United Kingdom. *J R Coll Physicians Lond* 1996;**30**:119–21.
3   Andrews K, Murphy L, Munday R, Littlewood C. Misdiagnosis of persistent vegative state. *Br Med j* 1996;**313**:13–6.

Source: *Journal of the Royal College of Physicians of London* Vol 31 No 3 May/June 1997.

3   Practice Note

THE OFFICIAL SOLICITOR: APPOINTMENT IN FAMILY PROCEEDINGS

(1) This note supersedes the previous practices notes published at [1993] 2 FLR 641 and [1995] 2 FLR 479. Its purpose is to provide fresh guidance on the appointment of the Official Solicitor.

Appointment as guardian ad litem of child subject to proceedings

Private law proceedings
(2) In non-specified (private law) proceedings under the Children Act 1989, and in proceedings under the inherent jurisdiction of the High Court, the Official Solicitor may act either in the High Court or in a county court (but not in a family proceedings court), under r 9.5 of the Family Proceedings Rules 1991 (SI 1991/1247). It is only where, in accordance with r 9.5, it appears to the court that the child ought to have party status and be separately represented that the question of the appointment of the Official Solicitor may arise.

(3) It most private law cases a child's interests will be sufficiently safeguarded by a court welfare officer's report. Care should be taken to avoid duplication by the Official Solicitor of the inquiries already conducted by the welfare officer (see *Re S (A Minor) (Guardian ad Litem/Welfare Officer)* [1993] 1 FLR 110). Reference to the Official Solicitor is likely to be warranted in cases where:

(a)   there is a significant foreign element such as a challenge to the English court's jurisdiction or a need for inquiries to be conducted abroad;
(b)   there is conflicting or controversial medical evidence, and the court considers that it would be appropriate to give leave for further medical evidence to be adduced;
(c)   there is a need for expert evidence which cannot be obtained by the parties jointly instructing an appropriate expert in accordance with *Re K (Contact: Psychiatric Report)* [1995] 2 FLR 432, and Children Act Advisory Committee *Handbook of Best Practice in Children Act Cases* (Lord Chancellor's Department, 1997), para 64 in the following circumstances:
   (i)   a child is ignorant of the truth as to its parentage;
   (ii)   a psychiatric assessment is required in relation to a child who is refusing contact with a parent;
(d)   an application is made for leave to seek contact with an adopted child (the procedure is set out in *Re C (A Minor) (Adopted Child: Contact)* [1993] Fam 210, [1993] 2 FLR 431);
(e)   the Official Solicitor is acting or is likely to be required to act for the child in other proceedings, for instance proceedings arising from the death of a parent, or where there are children from different families who fail to be represented in linked proceedings, such as paedophile ring cases;
(f)   there are exceptionally difficult, unusual or sensitive issues; such cases will be likely to be High Court matters.

(4) The Official Solicitor will almost invariably accept appointment in cases where judicial guidance has been given about his appointment, that is to say:

(a)   where a child wants to instruct a solicitor direct but the court does not consider he is competent (see *Re T (A Minor) (Wardship: Representation)* [1994] Fam 49, [1993] 2 FLR 278 – see also para (8) below). If a child has been granted leave pursuant to Family Proceedings Rules 1991, r 9.2A to instruct a solicitor but the court needs the assistance of the Official Solicitor as guardian ad litem then he will normally be prepared to act (r 9.2A(6A));
(b)   in 'special category' medical treatment cases, such a sterilisation and vegetative state cases, and cases involving children actually or potentially refusing medical treatment. Applications in such cases should be made under the inherent jurisdiction of the High Court.

Public law proceedings
(5) The Official Solicitor may only be appointed in the High Court, and in accordance with *Practice Direction: Lord Chancellor's Direction: Duties and Functions of the Official Solicitor under the Children Act 1989* (7 October 1991) [1991] 2 FLR 471, where the court considers that the circumstances are that:

(a)   the child does not have a guardian ad litem in the proceedings; and
(b)   there are exceptional circumstances which make it desirable in the interests of the welfare of the child concerned that the Official Solicitor, rather than a panel guardian should be appointed, having regard to:
       (i)   any foreign element in the case which is likely to require inquiries, or other action, to be pursued outside England and Wales;
       (ii)   the burden of having to represent several children;
       (iii) other High Court proceedings in which the Official Solicitor is representing the child;
       (iv)   any other circumstances which the court considers relevant.

(6) The Official Solicitor, in accordance with the direction, may also give informal advice and other assistance as he considers appropriate to any guardian ad litem in specified proceedings in the High Court. The court will be very slow to remove a panel guardian ad litem already substantially involved in a case. It is open to the court to retain the panel guardian and invite the Official Solicitor to act as amicus curiae to conduct particular legal inquiries or carry out other duties which the panel guardian and solicitor cannot be expected to undertake.

Adoption
(7) Provision for the appointment of the Official Solicitor as the child's guardian ad litem in adoption and freeing for adoption proceedings in the High Court is to be found at rr 6(4) and 18(4) of the Adoption Rules 1984 (SI 1984/265). As a general rule, the Official Solicitor can be expected to accept the appointment as the child's guardian ad litem in contested applications under the 1976 Act, although where the adoption or freeing proceedings follow on from former public law proceedings, the likelihood is that the child's former guardian ad litem will be a more appropriate candidate. With certain exceptions, which are noted in *Practice Direction (Adoption: Ward of Court)* (25 June 1986) [1986] 1 WLR 933, the Official Solicitor is unlikely to accept appointment as the

child's guardian ad litem in adoption or freeing for adoption applications which are expected to proceed with the agreement of the birth parent.

Appointment as next friend and for child not subject of proceedings
(8) Subject to his being satisfied that the proposed proceedings would benefit the child, the Official Solicitor may also act as next friend of a child seeking leave to make an application (typically for sibling contact) under Children Act 1989, s 10(8). The Official Solicitor may also accept appointment under r 9.2(1) in respect of any minor who is a party to family proceedings, such as a minor mother of a child who is the subject of the proceedings. Minor parents, as well as children who are the subject of the proceedings, may invoke r 9.2A if they wish to instruct a solicitor directly.

Appointment as guardian ad litem of an adult party under disability
(9) In the absence of any other suitable and willing person, the Official Solicitor is available to be appointed, in the High Court or in a county court pursuant to Family Proceedings Rules 1991, r 9.2(1) as the guardian ad litem or next friend of an adult party to family proceedings who is a patient. The term 'patient' means someone who is incapable by reason of mental disorder within the meaning of s 1 of the Mental Health Act 1983 of managing and administering his property and affairs. Medical evidence will usually be required before the Official Solicitor can act as his staff can provide a standard form of medical certificate. Where there are practical difficulties in obtaining such medical evidence, the Official Solicitor should be consulted.

Terms of appointment
(10) Orders appointing the Official Solicitor should be expressed as being made subject to his consent. Save in the most urgent of cases, a substantive hearing date less than 3 months ahead should not be fixed without consulting his office. It is often helpful to discuss the question of appointment with the Official Solicitor or one of his staff by telephoning 0171 911 7127.

(11) The following documents should be forwarded to the Official Solicitor without delay:

(a)   a copy of the order appointing him (subject to his consent) and a note of the reasons approved by the judge;
(b)   the court file;
(c)   wherever practicable, a chronology and a statement of issues.

THE OFFICIAL SOLICITOR CANNOT DECIDE WHETHER TO ACCEPT APPOINTMENT UNTIL HE HAS RECEIVED THESE DOCUMENTS.

The Official Solicitor's address is:

81 Chancery Lane
London, WC2A 1DD
DX 0012 London/Chancery Lane
Fax 0171 911 7105

December 1998

PETER HARRIS
Official Solicitor

4　Practice Note

OFFICIAL SOLICITOR TO THE SUPREME COURT: VEGETATIVE STATE

The need for the prior sanction of a High Court judge
(1)   The termination of artificial feeding and hydration for patients in a vegetative state will in virtually all cases require the prior sanction of a High Court judge: *Airedale NHS Trust v Bland* [1993] AC 789, 805 per Sir Stephen Brown P, and *Frenchay Healthcare NHS Trust v S* [1994] 1 FLR 485.

(2)   The diagnosis should be made in accordance with the most up-to-date generally accepted guidelines for the medical profession. A working group of the Royal College of Physicians issued guidance on the diagnosis and management of the permanent vegetative state (PVS) in March 1996 ((1996) 30 J R Coll Physns 119–21). This has been endorsed by the Conference of Medical Royal Colleges. The working group advises that the diagnosis of PVS is not absolute but based on probabilities. Such a diagnosis may not reasonably be made until the patient has been in a continuing vegetative state following head injury for more than 12 months or following other causes of brain damage for more than 6 months. Before then, as soon as the patient's condition has stabilised, rehabilitative measures such as coma arousal programmes, should be instituted (see *Airedale NHS Trust v Bland* at 870–871 per Lord Goff). It is not appropriate to apply to court for permission to terminate artificial feeding and hydration until the condition is judged to be permanent. In many cases it will be necessary to commission reports based on clinical and other observations of the patient over a period of time.

Applications to court
(3)   Applications to court should be by originating summons issued in the Family Division of the High Court seeking a declaration in the form set out in para (5) below. Subject to specific provisions below, the application should follow the procedure laid down for sterilisation cases by the House of Lords in *Re F (Mental Patient: Sterilisation)* [1990] 2 AC 1, [1989] 2 FLR 376 and in the *Practice Note – Official Solicitor: Sterilisation (June 1996)* [1996] 2 FLR 111.

(4)   Applications to court in relation to minors should be made within wardship proceedings. In such cases the applicant should seek the leave of the court for the termination of feeding and hydration, rather than a declaration. The form of relief set out in para (5) below should be amended accordingly.

(5)   The originating summons should seek relief in the following form:

　'(1)   It is declared that despite the inability of X to give a valid consent, the plaintiffs and/or the responsible medical practitioners:
　　(i)　may lawfully discontinue all life-sustaining treatment and medical support measures (including ventilation, nutrition and hydration by artificial means) designed to keep X alive in his existing permanent vegetative state; and

      (ii)   may lawfully furnish such treatment and nursing care whether at hospital or elsewhere under medical supervision as may be appropriate to ensure X suffers the least distress and retains the greatest dignity until such time as his life comes to an end.

   (2)   It is ordered that in the event of a material change in the existing circumstances occurring before such withdrawal of treatment any party shall have liberty to apply for such further or other declaration or order as may be just.'

(6)   The case will normally be heard in open court. The court will, however, usually take steps to preserve the anonymity of the patient and the patient's family (and, where appropriate, the hospital) by making orders under s 11 of the Contempt of Court Act 1981: *Re G (Adult Patient: Publicity)* [1995] 2 FLR 528. An order restricting publicity will continue to have effect notwithstanding the death of the patient, unless and until an application is made to discharge it: *Re C (Adult Patient: Publicity)* [1996] 2 FLR 251).

The parties
(7)   The applicant may be either the next of kin or other individual closely connected with the patient or the relevant district health authority/NHS trust (which, in any event, ought to be a party): *Re S (Hospital Patient: Court's Jurisdiction)* [1996] Fam 1, CA). The views of the next-of-kin or of others close to the patient cannot act as a veto to an application but they must be taken fully into account by the court: *Re G (Persistent Vegetative State)* [1995] 2 FCR 46.

(8)   The Official Solicitor should normally be invited to act as guardian ad litem of the patient, who will inevitably be a patient within the meaning of RSC Ord 80. In any case in which the Official Solicitor does not represent the patient, he should be joined as a defendant or respondent.

The investigation
(9)   There should be at least two independent reports on the patient from neurologists or other doctors experienced in assessing disturbances of consciousness. One of these reports will be commissioned by the Official Solicitor. The duties of doctors making the diagnosis are described in the report of the working group of the Royal College of Physicians as follows:

'They should undertake their own assessment separately and should write clearly the details of that assessment and their conclusion in the notes. The medical practitioners shall separately perform a formal neurological examination and consider the results of those investigations which have been undertaken to identify the cause of the condition. It is helpful for nursing staff and relatives to be present during the examination; their role as responsible witnesses who spend a much longer time with the patient than can the medical practitioners must be recognised.

It is to be emphasised that there is no urgency in making the diagnosis of the permanent vegetative state. If there is any uncertainty in the mind of the assessor then the diagnosis shall not be made and a reassessment undertaken after further time has elapsed. The most important role of the medical practitioner in making the diagnosis is to ensure that the patient is not sentient and, in this respect, the views of the nursing staff, relatives and carers are of considerable importance and help.'

The views of the patient and others

(10)   The Official Solicitor's representative will normally require to interview the next-of-kin and others close to the patient as well as seeing the patient and those caring for him. The views of the patient may have been previously expressed, either in writing or otherwise. The High Court may determine the effect of a purported advance directive as to future medical treatment: *Re T (Adult: Refusal of Medical Treatment)* [1993] Fam 95, sub nom *Re T (An Adult) (Consent to Medical Treatment)* [1992] 2 FLR 458; *Re C (Refusal of Medical Treatment)* [1994] 1 FLR 31. In summary, the patient's previously expressed views, if any, will always be an important component in the decisions of the doctors and the court, particularly if they are clearly established and were intended to apply to the circumstances which have in fact arisen.

Consultation with the Official Solicitor

(11)   Members of the Official Solicitor's legal staff are prepared to discuss PVS cases before proceedings have been issued. Contact with the Official Solicitor may be made by telephoning 0171 911 7127 during office hours.

(12)   This Practice Note replaces the Practice Note dated March 1994 reported at [1994] 1 FLR 654.

26 July 1996   PETER HARRIS
                                                                                                    Official Solicitor

5   Practice Note

OFFICIAL SOLICITOR: STERILISATION

The need for the prior sanction of a High Court judge
1. The sterilisation of a minor or a mentally incompetent adult ('the patient') will in virtually all cases require the prior sanction of a High Court judge: *Re B (A Minor) (Wardship: Sterilisation)* [1988] AC 199, [1987] 2 FLR 314; *Re F (Sterilisation: Mental Patient)* [1990] 2 AC 1, [1989] 2 FLR 376.

Applications to court
2. Applications in respect of a minor should be made in the Family Division of the High Court, within proceedings either under the inherent jurisdiction of s 8(1) ('a specific issue order') of the Children Act 1989. In the Official Solicitor's view, the procedural and administrative difficulties attaching to applications under s 8 of the Children Act 1989 are such that the preferred course is to apply within the inherent jurisdiction.

3. Within the inherent jurisdiction, applicants should seek an order in the following or a broadly similar form:

'It is ordered that there be leave to perform an operation of sterilisation on the minor [X] *[if it is desired to specify the precise method of carrying out the operation add, for example, by the occlusion of her fallopian tubes]* and to carry out such post-operative treatment and care as may be necessary in her best interests.'

4. Applications in respect of an adult should be by way of originating summons in the Family Division of the High Court for an order in the following or a broadly similar form:

'It is declared that the operation of sterilisation proposed to be performed on [X] *[if it is desired to specify the precise method of carrying out the operation, add, for example, by the occlusion of her fallopian tubes]* being in the existing circumstances in her best interests can lawfully be performed on her despite her inability to consent to it.

It is ordered that in the event of a material change in the existing circumstances occurring before the said operation has been performed any party shall have liberty to apply for such further or other declaration or order as may be just.'

The parties
5. The plaintiff or applicant should normally be a parent or one of those responsible for the care of the patient or those intending to carry out the proposed operation. The patient must always be a party and should normally be a defendant (or respondent). In cases in which the patient is a defendant the patient's guardian ad litem should normally be the Official Solicitor. In any case in which the Official Solicitor does not represent the patient he should be a defendant.

Procedure
6. There will in every case be a hearing before a High Court judge fixed for directions on the first open date after the passage of 8 weeks from the issue of the originating summons.

7. The case will normally be heard in chambers. If it is heard in open court, the court will usually take steps to preserve the anonymity of the patient and the patient's family by making appropriate orders under the Contempt of Court Act 1981: *Re G (Adult Patient: Publicity)* [1995] 2 FLR 528.

Evidence
8. The purpose of the proceedings is to establish whether or not the proposed sterilisation is in the best interests of the patient. The judge will require to be satisfied that those proposing sterilisation are seeking it in good faith and that their paramount concern is for the best interests of the patient rather than their own or the public's convenience. The proceedings will normally involve a thorough adversarial investigation of all possible viewpoints and any possible alternatives to sterilisation. Nevertheless, straightforward cases proceeding without dissent may be disposed of at the hearing for directions without oral evidence.

9. The Official Solicitor will in all cases, in whichever capacity he acts, carry out his own investigations, call his own witnesses and take whatever other steps appear to him to be necessary in order to ensure that all medical psychological and social evaluations are conducted and that all relevant matters are properly canvassed before the court. Expert and other witnesses called in support of the proposed operation will be cross-examined and all reasonable arguments presented against sterilisation. The Official Solicitor will require to meet and interview the patient in private in all cases where he or she is able to express any views (however limited) about the case.

10. The Official Solicitor anticipates that the court will particularly require evidence clearly establishing the following:

Mental capacity
(1)   That the patient is incapable of making her own decision about sterilisation and is unlikely to develop sufficiently to make an informed judgment about sterilisation in the foreseeable future, having regard to the most up-to-date medical knowledge in this field. In this connection it must be borne in mind that—

(i)   the fact that a person is legally incompetent for some purposes does not mean that she necessarily lacks the capacity to make a decision about sterilisation; and
(ii)   in the case of a minor her youth and potential for development may make it difficult or impossible to make the relevant finding of incapacity.

Risk of pregnancy
(2)   That there is a need for contraception because the patient is fertile and is sexually active or is likely to engage in sexual activity in the foreseeable future. (*Re W (Mental Patient: Sterilisation)* [1993] 1 FLR 381.)

Potential psychological damage
(3)   That the patient is likely if she becomes pregnant or gives birth to experience substantial trauma or psychological damage greater than that resulting from the sterilisation itself.

Alternative methods of contraception
(4)   That there is no appropriate reversible method of contraception available having regard to the most up-to-date medical knowledge in this field.

Consultation

11. Members of the Official Solicitor's legal staff are prepared to discuss sterilisation cases before proceedings have been issued. Contact with the Official Solicitor may be made by telephoning 0171 911 7127 during office hours.

June 1996   **Official Solicitor**

This note replaces the Practice Notes reported at [1989] 2 FLR 447, [1990] 2 FLR 530 and [1993] 2 FLR 222.

6   Decisions relating to cardiopulmonary resuscitation

A STATEMENT FROM THE BMA AND RCN IN ASSOCIATION WITH THE RESUSCITATION COUNCIL (UK)

Note: *At the date of publication, it is anticipated that the following statement will be subject to imminent change. If readers require information concerning the proposed changes, they should request further information from the address appearing at the end of the statement.*

Introduction

Cardiopulmonary Resuscitation (CPR) can be attempted on any individual in whom cardiac or respiratory function ceases. Such events are inevitable as part of dying and thus CPR can theoretically be used on every individual prior to death. It is therefore essential to identify patients for whom cardiopulmonary arrest represents a terminal event in their illness and in whom CPR is inappropriate.

Background

'Do-not-resuscitate' (DNR) orders may be a potent source of misunderstanding and dissent amongst doctors, nurses and others involved in care of patients. Many of the problems in this difficult area would be avoided if communication and explanation of the decision were improved.

A letter from the Chief Medical Officer (PL/CMO (91) 22) following a case brought to the attention of the Health Service Commissioner has clarified where responsibility lies. The Chief Medical Officer makes it clear that the responsibility for resuscitation policy lies with the consultant concerned and that each consultant should ensure that this policy is understood by all staff who may be involved and in particular junior medical staff. Unfortunately, in many cases discussion and consultation about the resuscitation of a patient is carried out by staff least experienced or equipped to undertake such sensitive tasks.

In a recent survey, the Royal College of Nursing found that most Health Authorities and Health Boards have taken steps to ensure that appropriate health workers are proficient in CPR. The problem of who should be resuscitated has not been addressed and several authorities stated they would welcome guidance. The factors surrounding a decision whether or not to initiate CPR involve complex clinical considerations and emotional issues. The decision arrived at in the care of one patient may be inappropriate in a superficially similar case.

These guidelines therefore should be viewed as a framework providing basic principles within which decisions regarding local policies on CPR may be formulated. Further assistance for doctors and nurses where individual problems arise, can be obtained from their respective professional organisations.

Guidelines

(1) It is appropriate to consider a do-not-resuscitate (DNR) decision in the following circumstances:

   (a) Where the patient's condition indicates that effective Cardiopulmonary Resuscitation (CPR) is unlikely to be successful.

   (b) Where CPR is not in accord with the recorded, sustained wishes of the patient who is mentally competent.

   (c) Where successful CPR is likely to be followed by a length and quality of life which would not be acceptable to the patient.

(2) Where a DNR order has not been made and the express wishes of the patient are unknown, resuscitation should be initiated if cardiac or pulmonary arrest occurs. Anyone initiating CPR in such circumstances should be supported by their senior medical and nursing colleagues.

(3) The overall responsibility for a DNR decision rests with the consultant in charge of the patient's care. This should be made after appropriate consultation and consideration of all aspects of the patient's condition. The perspectives of other members of the medical and nursing team, the patient, and with due regard to patient confidentiality, the patient's relatives or close friends, may all be valuable in forming the consultant's decision.

(4) Discussion of cardiopulmonary resuscitation with all patients would be inappropriate. However, there are circumstances in which sensitive exploration of the patient's wishes should be undertaken, ideally by the consultant concerned, for example, with patients who are at risk or cardiac or pulmonary failure or who have a terminal illness. Such discussions should be documented in the patient's record.

(5) Although responsibility for CPR policy rests with the consultant, he or she should be prepared always to discuss the decision for an individual patient with other health professionals involved in the patient's care.

(6) Proper understanding of the DNR order is impossible without knowing the rationale behind it. The entry in the medical records of the decision and reasons for it should be made by the most senior member of the medical team available who should ensure that the decision is effectively communicated to other members of staff.

(7) Recording in the nursing notes should be made by the primary nurse or the most senior member of the nursing team whose responsibility it is to inform other members of the nursing team.

(8) The decision reached following admission of the patient should be reviewed by the consultant in charge at the soonest available opportunity. Such decisions will, of necessity, need to be reviewed regularly in the light of changes in the patient's condition.

(9) When the basis for a DNR order is the absence of any likely medical benefit, discussion with the patient, or others close to the patient, should aim at securing an understanding and acceptance of the clinical decision that has been reached. If a DNR decision is based on quality of life considerations, the views of the patient where these can be ascertained are particularly important. If the patient cannot express a view, the opinion of family or others close to the patient may be sought regarding the patient's best interests.

(10) Discussions of the advisability or otherwise of CPR will be highly sensitive and complex and should be undertaken by senior and experienced members of the medical team supported by senior nursing colleagues. A DNR order applies solely to CPR. It should be made clear that all other treatment and care which are appropriate for the patient are not precluded and should not be influenced by a DNR order.

(11) Experience with DNR orders is an appropriate subject for clinical audit.

Requests for further information and all enquiries should be directed to the Medical Ethics Committee Secretariat, Ethics, Science and Information Division, BMA House.

British Medical Association
BMA House
Tavistock Square
LONDON WC1H 9JP

March 1993

7   Clauses 1 to 5 of a draft of a Bill annexed to the Law Commission Report No 231 on Mental Incapacity

PART I

MENTAL INCAPACITY

CHAPTER I

PRELIMINARY

1. Purpose of Part I

(1) This Part of this Act has effect –

    (a) for conferring statutory authority, subject to specified restrictions, for things done for the personal welfare or health care of a person without capacity; and

    (b) for enabling decisions to be made on behalf of such a person by the donee of a power of attorney (in this Act referred to as a 'continuing power of attorney') which complies with the requirements of this Part of this Act, by the court or by a manager appointed by the court.

(2) Except as otherwise provided, this Part of this Act does not enable anything to be done for, or a decision to be made on behalf of, a person who has not attained the age of sixteen.

2. Persons without capacity

(1) For the purposes of this Part of this Act a person is without capacity if at the material time –

    (a) he is unable by reason of mental disability to make a decision for himself on the matter in question; or

    (b) he is unable to communicate his decision on that matter because he is unconscious or for any other reason.

(2) For the purposes of this Part of this Act a person is at the material time unable to make a decision by reason of mental disability if the disability is such that at the time when the decision needs to be made –

    (a) he is unable to understand or retain the information relevant to the decision, including information about the reasonably foreseeable consequences of deciding one way or another or of failing to make the decision; or

    (b) he is unable to make a decision based on that information,

and in this Act 'mental disability' means a disability or disorder of the mind or brain, whether permanent or temporary, which results in an impairment or disturbance of mental functioning.

(3) A person shall not be regarded as unable to understand the information referred to in subsection (2)(a) above if he is able to understand an explanation of that information in broad terms and in simple language.

(4) A person shall not be regarded as unable to make a decision by reason of mental disability merely because he makes a decision which would not be made by a person of ordinary prudence.

(5) A person shall not be regarded as unable to communicate his decision unless all practicable steps to enable him to do so have been taken without success.

(6) There shall be a presumption against lack of capacity and any question whether a person lacks capacity shall be decided on the balance of probabilities.

3. Actions to be in best interests of persons without capacity

(1) Anything done for, and any decision made on behalf of, a person by virtue of this Part of this Act shall be done or made in his best interests.

(2) In deciding what is in a person's best interests regard shall be had to the following –

    (a) so far as ascertainable, his past and present wishes and feelings and the factors which he would consider if he were able to do so;

    (b) the need to permit and encourage that person to participate, or to improve his ability to participate, as fully as possible in anything done for and any decision affecting him;

    (c) if it is practicable and appropriate to consult them, the views as to that person's wishes and feelings and as to what would be in his best interests of –

        (i) any person named by him as someone to be consulted on those matters;

        (ii) anyone (whether his spouse, a relative, friend or other person) enaged in caring for him or interested in his welfare;

        (iii) the donee of any continuing power of attorney granted by him;

        (iv) any manager appointed for him by the court;

    (d) whether the purpose for which any action or decision is required can be as effectively achieved in a manner less restrictive of his freedom of action.

(3) In the case of anything done or a decision made by a person other than the court it shall be a sufficient compliance with subsection (1) above if that person reasonably believes that what he does or decides is in the best interests of the person concerned.

CHAPTER II

CARE OF PERSON WITHOUT CAPACITY

General authority

4. Power to provide care

(1) Subject to the provisions of this Chapter, it shall be lawful to do anything for the personal welfare or health care of a person who is, or is reasonably believed to be, without capacity in relation to the matter in question ('the person concerned') if it is in all the circumstances reasonable for it to be done by the person who does it.

(2) Where what is done by virtue of this section involves expenditure it shall be lawful –

    (a) for that purpose to pledge the credit of the person concerned; and

    (b) to apply money in the possession of the person concerned for meeting the expenditure;

and if the expenditure is borne for him by another person that person shall be entitled to reimburse himself out of any such money or to be otherwise indemnified by the person concerned.

(3) Subsection (2) above is without prejudice to any power to spend money for the benefit of the person concerned which is exercisable apart from this section by virtue of having lawful control of money or other property of his.

(4) Schedule 1 to this Act shall have effect for enabling certain payments which would otherwise be made to a person without capacity to be made instead to a person acting on his behalf or to be otherwise dealt with as provided in that Schedule.

Restrictions on general authority

5. No powers of coercion

(1) Subject to subsection (2) below, section 4 above does not authorise –

    (a) the use or threat of force to enforce the doing of anything to which the person concerned objects; or

    (b) the detention or confinement of that person whether or not he objects.

(2) This section does not preclude the taking of any steps necessary to avert a substantial risk of serious harm to the person concerned.

8 Guidelines laid down by the Court of Appeal in *St George's Healthcare NHS Trust v S* [1998] 2 FLR 728 at 758 as applicable in circumstances where there is serious doubt as to an adult patient's capacity to accept or decline medical treatment

---

30 July 1998

[On 30 July 1998 the following guidelines were handed down in open court:]

Guidelines

The case highlighted some major problems which could arise for hospital authorities when a pregnant woman presented at hospital, the possible need for Caesarean surgery was diagnosed, and there was serious doubt about the patient's capacity to accept or decline treatment. To avoid any recurrence of the unsatisfactory events recorded in this judgment, and after consultation with the President of the Family Division and the Official Solicitor, and in the light of written submissions from Mr Havers and Mr Gordon, we shall attempt to repeat and expand the advice given in *Re MB (Medical Treatment)* [1997] 2 FLR 426. This advice also applies to any cases involving capacity when surgical or invasive treatment may be needed by a patient, whether female or male. References to 'she' and 'he' should be read accordingly. It also extends, where relevant, to medical practitioners and health practitioners generally as well as to hospital authorities.

The guidelines depend upon basic legal principles which we can summarise:

(i)   They have no application where the patient is competent to accept or refuse treatment. In principle a patient may remain competent notwithstanding detention under the Mental Health Act.

(ii) If the patient is competent and refuses consent to the treatment an application to the High Court for a declaration would be pointless. In this situation the advice given to the patient should be recorded. For their own protection hospital authorities should seek unequivocal assurances from the patient (to be recorded in writing) that the refusal represents an informed decision: that is, that she understands the nature of and reasons for the proposed treatment, and the risks and likely prognosis involved in the decision to refuse or accept it. If the patient is unwilling to sign a written indication of this refusal, this too should be noted in writing. Such a written indication is merely a record for evidential purposes. It should not be confused with or regarded as a disclaimer.

(iii) If the patient is incapable of giving or refusing consent, either in the long term or temporarily (eg due to unconsciousness), the patient must be cared for according to the authority's judgment of the patient's best interests. Where the patient has given an advance directive, before becoming incapable, treatment and care should normally be subject to the advice directive. However, if there is reason to doubt the reliability of the advance directive (for example it may sensibly be thought not to apply to the circumstances which have arisen) then an application for a declaration may be made.

Concern over capacity

(iv) The authority should identify as soon as possible whether there is concern about a patient's competence to consent to or refuse treatment.

(v) If the capacity of the patient is seriously in doubt it should be assessed as a matter of priority. In many such cases the patient's general practitioner or other responsible doctor may be sufficiently qualified to make the necessary assessment, but in serious or complex cases involving difficult issues about the future health and well-being or even life of the patient, the issue of capacity should be examined by an independent psychiatrist, ideally one approved under s 12(2) of the Mental Health Act. If following this assessment there remains a serious doubt about the patient's competence, and the seriousness or complexity of the issues in the particular case may require the involvement of the court, the psychiatrist should further consider whether the patient is incapable by reason of mental disorder of managing her property or affairs. If so the patient may be unable to instruct a solicitor and will require a guardian ad litem in any court proceedings. The authority should seek legal advice as quickly as possible. If a declaration is to be sought the patient's solicitors should be informed immediately and if practicable they should have a proper opportunity to take instructions and apply for legal aid where necessary. Potential witnesses for the authority should be made aware of the criteria laid down in *Re MB* and this case, together with any guidance issued by the Department of Health, and the British Medical Association.

(vi) If the patient is unwilling to instruct solicitors, or is believed to be incapable of doing so, the authority or its legal advisors must notify the Official Solicitor and invite him to act as guardian ad litem. If the Official Solicitor agrees he will no doubt wish, if possible, to arrange for the patient to be interviewed to ascertain her wishes and to explore the reasons for any refusal of treatment. The Official Solicitor can be contacted through the Urgent Court Business Officer out of office hours on 0171 936 6000.

The hearing

(vii) The hearing before the judge should be inter partes. As the order made in her absence will not be binding on the patient unless she is represented either by a guardian ad litem (if incapable of giving instructions) or (if capable) by counsel or solicitor, a declaration granted ex parte is of no assistance to the authority. Although the Official Solicitor will not act for a patient if she is capable of instructing a solicitor, the court may in any event call on the Official Solicitor (who has considerable expertise in these matters) to assist as an amicus curiae.

(viii)It is axiomatic that the judge must be provided with accurate and all the relevant information. This should include the reasons for the proposed treatment, the risks involved in the proposed treatment, and in not proceeding with it, whether any alternative treatment exists, and the reason, if ascertainable, why the patient is refusing the proposed treatment. The judge will need sufficient information to reach an informed conclusion about the patient's capacity, and, where it arises, the issue of best interest.

(ix)   The precise terms of any order should be recorded and approved by the judge before its terms are transmitted to the authority. The patient should be accurately informed of the precise terms.

(x)   Applicants for emergency orders from the High Court made without first issuing and serving the relevant applications and evidence in support have a duty to comply with the procedural requirements (and pay the court fees) as soon as possible after the emergency hearing.

Conclusion

There may be occasions when, assuming a serious question arises about the competence of the patient, the situation facing the authority may be so urgent and the consequences so desperate that it is impracticable to attempt to comply with these guidelines. The guidelines should be approached for what they are, that is, guidelines. Where delay may itself cause serious damage to the patient's health or put her life at risk then formulaic compliance with these guidelines would be inappropriate.

9 Advance statements about medical treatment

CODE OF PRACTICE

Report of the British Medical Association

PART I

Background

1 Introduction

1.1 This Code reflects good clinical practice in encouraging dialogue about individuals' wishes concerning their future treatment. It does not address euthanasia, assisted suicide or methods for allocating health service resources. These are entirely separate from advance statements.

1.2 At all stages of life, timely discussion of treatment options is an important part of the duty of care owed by health professionals to those who consult them. Recognising and respecting the individual patient's values and preferences are fundamental aspects of good practice.

2 Definitions

2.1 *Advance statements:* People who understand the implications of their choices can state in advance how they wish to be treated if they suffer loss of mental capacity. Just as adults must be consulted about treatment options, young people under the age of majority (age 18) are entitled to have their views taken into account. An advance statement (sometimes known as a living will) can be of various types.

– a requesting statement reflecting an individual's aspirations and preferences. This can help health professionals identify how the person would like to be treated without binding them to that course of action, if it conflicts with professional judgement.*

– a statement of the general beliefs and aspects of life which an individual values. This provides a summary of individual responses to a list of questions about a person's past and present wishes and future desires. It makes no specific request or refusal but attempts to give a biographical portrait of the individual as an aid to deciding what he or she would want.

– a statement which names another person who should be consulted at the time a decision has to be made. The views expressed by that named person should reflect what the patient would want. This can supplement and clarify the intended scope of a written statement but the named person's views are presently not legally binding in England & Wales. In Scotland, the powers of a tutor dative may cover such eventualities.

–   a clear instruction refusing some or all medical procedures (advance directive). Made by a competent adult, this does, in certain circumstances, have legal force.

–   a statement which, rather than refusing any particular treatment, specifies a degree of irreversible deterioration (such as a diagnosis of persistent vegetative state) after which no life sustaining treatment should be given. For adults, this again can have legal force.

–   a combination of the above, including requests, refusals and the nomination of a representative. Those sections expressing clear refusal may have legal force in the case of adult patients.

2.2   *Advance directives* (refusals): Competent, informed adults have an established legal right to refuse medical procedures in advance. **An unambiguous and informed advance refusal is as valid as a contemporaneous decision. Health professionals are bound to comply when the refusal specifically addresses the situation which has arisen.** Refusal is a serious matter, ideally to be considered in discussion with health professionals.

Since no one can demand that medical treatment be given, statements purporting to 'direct' or instruct health professionals are necessarily refusals. Although a clear refusal is potentially legally binding, a refusal seriously likely to affect other people adversely (such as exposing them to the risk of harm) may be invalidated. This includes a refusal of basic care measures.

2.3   *Care:* Basic care means those procedures essential to keep an individual comfortable. The administration of medication or the performance of any procedure which is **solely or primarily** designed to provide comfort to the patient or alleviate that person's pain, symptoms or distress are facets of basic care. In each case, health professionals must continually assess the scope of measures essential for the patient's comfort. Although the law on this matter is not clear, this Code provides that as a matter of public policy, people should not be able to refuse basic care in advance or instruct others to refuse it on their behalf (see also section 5).

2.4   *Capacity:* Indicates an ability to understand the implications of the particular decision which the individual purports to make. The High Court has held that a person has capacity if he or she can understand and retain the information relevant to the decision in question, can believe that information and can weigh that information in the balance to arrive at a choice. (For assessment of capacity, see section 8.)

PART II

Making Treatment Choices

3.1   Adults can refuse clinical procedures contemporaneously or in advance of deteriorating mental capacity. Although no parallel right to insist upon a specific procedure or to order one of various treatment options is recognised in law, dialogue with patients about the choices facing them is an essential part of ethical health-care. Patients may properly expect to be provided with the details they need in an accessible form to allow them to make informed choices.

3.2   Discussion of options should be responsive to a patient's actual anxieties rather than trying to shape the patient's wishes to a preconceived standard format.

3.3   Many personal, non-clinical issues influence how competent people reach decisions. When decisions are made on behalf of people who cannot choose for themselves, their previously expressed wishes and values should be taken into account.

3.4   An advance directive is not restricted to care in hospital. It may also cover care at home, in a nursing home or in a hospice.

4   The Legal Position

4.1   Common law establishes that an informed refusal of treatment made in advance by an adult who understands the implications of that decision has the same legal power as a contemporaneous refusal. In order to be legally binding, the individual must have envisaged the type of situation which has subsequently arisen. In all circumstances, a contemporaneous decision by a competent individual overrides previously expressed statements by that person.

4.2   Young people under the age of majority do not have the same rights at law as adults. It is good practice, however, for children and young people to be kept as fully informed as possible about their care and treatment. The Children Act 1989 emphasises that the views of minors should be sought and taken into account in matters which touch on their welfare. Where appropriate, they should be encouraged to take decisions jointly with those with whom they have a close relationship, especially parents.

4.3   Advance statements are not covered by legislation. In cases of conflict with other legal provisions, advance statements are superseded by existing statute. The terms of the Mental Health Acts take precedence and must prevail regarding treatment for mental disorder. A compulsorily detained adult can make a legally binding advance refusal of treatment **not** covered by the mental health legislation. Where appropriate, patients' preferences should be included in treatment plans for both informal and detained patients.

5   Public Policy

5.1   Advance statements refusing basic care and maintenance of an incompetent person's comfort should not, as a matter of public policy, be binding on care providers. Although the law on this matter is not free from doubt, this Code provides that people should not be able to refuse basic care in advance or instruct others to refuse it on their behalf.

5.2   In the absence of an advance statement by a person who is now incapable of deciding, health professionals have a duty to act in that person's best interests.

5.3   Relatives' views may help in clarifying a patient's wishes but relatives' opinions cannot overrule those of the patient or supplant health professionals' duty to assess the patient's best interests.

PART III

Drafting

6   Making an Advance Statement

6.1   Although oral statements are equally valid if supported by appropriate evidence, there are advantages to recording one's general views and firm decisions in writing. Advance statements should be understood as an aid to, rather than a substitute for, open dialogue between patients and health professionals.

6.2   Written statements should use clear and unambiguous language. They should be signed by the individual and a witness. Model forms are available but clear statements in any format command respect.

6.3   Patients have a legitimate expectation of being provided with information in an accessible form to allow them to make informed choices. Health professionals should ensure that the foreseeable options and implications are adequately explained, admit to uncertainty when this is the case and make reasonable efforts to discover if there is more specialised information available to pass on to the patient. An open attitude on the part of health professionals and a willingness to discuss the advantages and disadvantages of certain options can do much to establish trust and mutual understanding.

6.4   Admittance to hospital, with its associated anxieties, is not generally a good time to raise the subject of anticipatory choice. Exceptions arise when the impetus for discussion comes from the patient or when sensitive advance discussion of cardiopulmonary resuscitation would be appropriate.

6.5   Advance statements should not be made under pressure. Professionals consulted at the drafting stage should take reasonable steps to ensure patients' decisions are not made under duress. Statements may evolve in stages over a period of time and discussion. It is inadvisable to conclude refusals or complicated statements in one discussion without further review. Patients should be reminded about the desirability of reviewing their statement on a regular basis, although a statement made long in advance is not automatically invalidated.

6.6   Patients should be advised to avoid rushing into specifying future treatment when they have only recently received a prognosis or when they may be unduly influenced by others or depressed.

6.7   Hospital managers and GP practice managers need to consider how to respond to the increasing desire by patients to plan ahead on the basis of accurate health information and advice.

6.8   When responding to a request for assistance with advance statements, there are fundamental issues health professionals should consider:

–   Does the patient have sufficient knowledge of the medical condition and possible treatment options if there is a known illness?

–   Is the patient mentally competent?

–   Is it clear that the patient is reflecting his or her own views and is not being pressured by other people?

6.9   There are advantages and disadvantages to making anticipatory decisions. Advance refusals are likely to be legally binding. Health professionals should try to ensure that patients are aware of drawbacks as well as advantages.

7   Contents of Advance Statements

7.1   Advance statements may list the individual's values as a basis for others to reach appropriate decisions. They may request all medically reasonable efforts be made to prolong life or express preferences between treatment options.

7.2   Advance directives are specific refusals of treatment and can be legally binding (see section 4).

7.3   Adults cannot authorise or refuse in advance, procedures which they could not authorise or refuse contemporaneously. They cannot authorise unlawful procedures or insist upon futile or inappropriate treatment.

7.4   Women of child bearing age should be advised to consider the possibility of their advance statement or directive being invoked at a time when they are pregnant. A waiver covering pregnancy might be written into the statement.

7.5   If a patient is detained under the Mental Health Act, drugs with potentially damaging side effects may sometimes have to be prescribed without prior discussion with the patient. When the patient regains insight, advance statements about preferences between equally viable options for future treatment can be discussed and reflected in subsequent treatment plans.

8   Assessing Mental Capacity

8.1   Opportunities for assessing mental capacity arise at two points. First, an individual must have enough understanding of the implications in order to make a valid advance statement. Secondly, that statement will then speak for the patient at the point where he or she is considered to have insufficient understanding to make the particular decision in question.

8.2   When consulted by someone who wishes to draft an advance statement, health professionals should consider whether there are any reasons to doubt the patient's capacity to make the decisions in question. Capacity is assumed unless evidence suggests the contrary. The signature of a health professional as a witness may well imply that assessment of capacity has taken place.

8.3   The High Court has held that a person has capacity if he or she can understand and retain the information relevant to the decision in question, can believe that information and can assess it in arriving at a choice.

8.4   To demonstrate capacity individuals should be able to:

–   understand in broad terms and simple language what the medical treatment is, its purpose and nature and why it is or will be proposed for them;

–   understand its principal benefits, risks and alternatives;

–   understand in broad terms what will be the consequences of not receiving the proposed treatment;

–   make a free choice (ie free from undue pressure);

–   retain the information long enough to make an effective decision.

9   Storage of Advance Statements

9.1   Storage of an advance statement and notification of its existence are primarily the responsibility of the individual. A copy of any written advance statement should be given to a person's General Practitioner. People close to the patient should be made aware of the existence of an advance statement and be told where it is.

9.2   For chronically ill patients, who are treated by a specialist team over a prolonged period, a copy of the advance statement should be in all relevant hospital files and the GP record.

PART IV

Implementation

10   General Implementation

10.1   If health professionals know or have reasonable grounds to believe that an advance statement exists and time permits, they should make further enquiries. This could be by looking in relevant hospital notes, or contacting the General Practitioner, or contacting people close to the patient.

10.2   Emergency treatment should not normally be delayed in order to look for an advance statement or refusal if there is no clear indication that one exists.

10.3   In England, Wales and Northern Ireland, no-one is legally empowered to consent or refuse on behalf of an adult who lacks capacity to make the particular treatment decision.

10.4   In Scotland, some treatment decisions may be taken by a tutor dative.

10.5   If an incapacitated pregnant woman presents with an apparently valid advance directive refusing treatment, legal advice should be sought to clarify the position.

10.6   One type of particularly serious condition is the persistent vegetative state (PVS) where there is no chance of recovery, but where life is dependent on artificial feeding. Diagnosis of this condition can be made only after twelve months when it is due to head injury but six months if it is due to other causes. The courts have to be consulted before treatment can be withdrawn and so any directive relating to PVS should be put before the courts before it can take effect.

10.7   If doubt exists about what the individual intends, the law supports a presumption in favour of providing clinically appropriate treatment. Carers and nurses during their working relationship with long-stay patients in residential or in-patient settings, are likely to have an understanding of the patient's feelings and opinions. Whilst these views should be taken into account they should not necessarily be determinative if in conflict with other evidence.

11 Liability of Health Professionals

11.1   Health professionals may be legally liable if they disregard the terms of an advance directive (ie refusal of treatment) if the directive is known of and applicable to the circumstances.

12 Disputes

12.1   In the event of disagreement between health professionals or between health professionals and people close to the patient, the senior clinician must consider the available evidence of the patient's wishes.

12.2   In cases of doubt or disagreement about the scope or validity of an advance directive (refusal), emergency treatment should normally be given and advice sought from the courts if the matter cannot be clarified in any other way.

12.3   In any case of dispute, legal judgment will be based upon the strength of the evidence.

13 Conscientious Objection

13.1   Some health professionals disagree in principle with patients' rights to refuse life-prolonging treatment but may nonetheless support advance statements which express preferences.

13.2   Health professionals are entitled to have their personal moral beliefs respected and not be pressurised to act contrary to those beliefs. But the 'sanctity of life' argument or other values must not be imposed upon those for whom they have or had no meaning.

13.3   Health professionals with a conscientious objection to limiting treatment at a patient's request should make their view clear when the patient initially raises the matter. In such cases the patient should be advised of the option of seeing another health professional if the patient wishes.

13.4   If a health professional is involved in the management of a case and cannot for reasons of conscience accede to a patient's request for limitation of treatment, management of that patient must be passed to a colleague.

13.5   In an emergency, if no other health professional is available there is a legal duty to comply with an appropriate and valid advance refusal.

PART V

Summary

14 Summary

14.1   Although not binding on health professionals, advance statements deserve thorough consideration and respect.

14.2   Where valid and applicable, advance directives (refusals) must be followed.

14.3   Health professionals consulted by people wishing to formulate an advance statement or directive should take all reasonable steps to provide accurate factual information about the treatment options and their implications.

14.4   Where an unknown and incapacitated patient presents for treatment some checks should be made concerning the validity of any directive refusing life-prolonging treatment. In all cases, it is vital to check that the statement or refusal presented is that of the patient being treated and has not been withdrawn.

14.5   If the situation is not identical to that described in the advance statement or refusal, treatment providers may still be guided by the general spirit of the statement if this is evident. It is advisable to contact any person nominated by the patient as well as the GP to clarify the patient's wishes. If there is doubt as to what the patient intended, the law requires the exercise of a best interests judgement.

14.6   If an incapacitated person is known to have had sustained and informed objections to all or some treatment, even though these have not been formally recorded, health professionals may not be justified in proceeding. This applies even in an emergency.

If witnessed and made at a time when the patient was competent and informed, such objections may constitute an oral advance directive. Health professionals will need to consider how much evidence is available about the patient's decisions and how convincing it seems. All members of the health care team can make a useful contribution to this process.

14.7   In the absence of any indication of the patient's wishes, there is a common law duty to give appropriate treatment to incapacitated patients when the treatment is clearly in their best interests.

Source: The Code of Practice is extracted from a booklet published by the British Medical Association under ISBN 0 7279 0914 2.

10 Living will

Living Will
Declaration

This is an important document. Before you fill it in, please read the notes which are attached to this form. We recommend that you discuss your Living Will with a doctor, but you do not have to.

Your name and address

Your name:

Your address:

I make this Living Will to record my wishes in case I become unable to communicate, and cannot take part in decisions about my medical care.

If you discuss this Living Will with a doctor before or after you fill it in, please fill in this section.

I have discussed this Living Will with the following doctor.

Doctor's name:

Doctor's address:

Doctor's phone number:

This form is the copyright of The Terrence Higgins Trust and Kings College London. Their permission is required in order to reproduce it.

Living Will
Advance Directives

1 – Medical treatment in general

Three possible health conditions are described below.

For each condition, choose 'A' or 'B' by ticking the appropriate box, or leave both boxes blank if you have no preference. The choice between 'A' and 'B' is exactly the same in each case.

Treat each case separately. You do not have to make the same choice for each one.

I declare that my wishes concerning medical treatment are as follows.

Case 1 – Life-threatening condition

Here are my wishes if:

- I have a physical illness from which there is no likelihood of recovery; *and*
- the illness is so serious that my life is nearing its end.

A I want to be kept alive for as long as is reasonably possible using whatever forms of medical treatment are available. ☐

B I do not want to be kept alive by medical treatment. I want medical treatment to be limited to keeping me comfortable and free from pain. I refuse all other medical treatment. ☐

Case 2 – Permanent mental impairment

Here are my wishes if:

- my mental functions have become permanently impaired;
- the impairment is so severe that I do not understand what is happening to me;
- there is no likelihood of improvement; *and*
- my physical condition then becomes so bad that I would need medical treatment to keep me alive.

A I want to be kept alive for as long as is reasonably possible using whatever forms of medical treatment are available. ☐

B I do not want to be kept alive by medical treatment. I want medical treatment to be limited to keeping me comfortable and free from pain. I refuse all other medical treatment. ☐

Case 3 – Permanent unconsciousness

Here are my wishes if:

- I become permanently unconscious and there is no likelihood I will regain consciousness.

A I want to be kept alive for as long as is reasonably possible using whatever forms of medical treatment are available. ☐

B I do not want to be kept alive by medical treatment. I want medical treatment to be limited to keeping me comfortable and free from pain. I refuse all other medical treatment. ☐

Living Will
Advance Directives

2 – Particular treatments or tests

If you have any wishes about particular medical treatments or tests, you can record them here. If you want to refuse a particular treatment or test, you should say so clearly. You should speak to a doctor before you write anything in this space.

I have the following wishes about particular medical treatments or tests.

3 – Having a friend or relative with you if your life is in danger

You can fill in this section if you would like a particular person to be with you if your life is in danger. It may not be possible to contact the person you name, or for him or her to arrive in time.

If my life is in danger, I want the following person to be contacted to give him or her a chance to be with me before I die.

Name:

Address:

Daytime phone number: **Evening phone number:**

Tick this box if you fill in a name in this section, and you want to be kept alive for as long as is reasonable to give the person you name a chance to reach you.

If you tick this box, any wishes you have stated above in Section 1 – *Medical treatment in general* and Section 2 - *Particular treatments or tests* may be **temporarily disregarded**. This is explained in the notes with this form.

Living Will
Health Care Proxy

I appoint the following person to take part in decisions about my medical care on my behalf and to represent my views about the decisions if I am unable to do so. I want him or her to be consulted about and involved in those decisions and I want anyone who is caring for me to respect the views he or she expresses on my behalf.

Name:

Address:

Daytime phone number:

Evening phone number:

This Living Will remains effective until I make clear that my wishes have changed.

Signatures

Sign and date the form here in the presence of a witness.

Date:

/   /

Your signature:

The witness must sign here after you have signed the form. The witness should then print his or her name and address in the spaces provided. Please read the notes to this form to see who should not be a witness.

Signature of witness:

Name of witness:

Address of witness:

This form is the copyright of The Terrence Higgins Trust and Kings College London. Their permission is required in order to reproduce it.

The Terrence Higgins Trust and the Centre of Medical Law and Ethics, King's College London developed this Living Will form.

We are a registered charity. We provide practical support, help, counselling and advice for anyone living with or concerned about AIDS and HIV infection.

The Terrence Higgins Trust
52-54 Grays Inn Road
London WC1X 8JU

Administration and advice centre
Phone: 0171 831 0330
Fax: 0171 242 0121

Charity Registration Number: 288527
Company Registration Number: 1778149
Registered in England
A company limited by guarantee

Helpline
0171 242 1010
12 noon to 10pm every day

Legal Line
0171 405 2381
7pm to 9pm on Monday and Wednesday

Our work is mainly supported
by voluntary donations.

The Centre of Medical Law and Ethics researches in and teaches all aspects of medical law, medical ethics and related public policy.

The Centre of Medical Law and Ethics
King's College London
Strand
London WC2R 2LS

THE QUEEN'S
ANNIVERSARY PRIZES
1996

Third edition April 1997
Copyright © 1997 The Terrence Higgins Trust and King's College London

You can reproduce this form for your personal use.
The form or extracts from it can also be reproduced or quoted by any publication to allow them to review or comment on it.
Any other person or organisation must get permission to reproduce the form from The Terrence Higgins Trust and King's College London.

We would like to thank the Lyndhurst Settlement for the financial help they gave us towards producing this form.

11 Medical directive/identity card for Jehovah's Witnesses

A. ADULTS

MEDICAL DOCUMENT

(see inside)

NO BLOOD

- -

IN CASE OF EMERGENCY, PLEASE CONTACT:

Name   Phone

Address

Name   Phone

Address

- -

Allergies:

Current medication:

Medical problems:

ADVANCE MEDICAL DIRECTIVE/RELEASE

I the undersigned   ,
born the   day of   19   , being one of
Jehovah's Witnesses with firm religious convictions have resolutely
decided to obey the Bible command "Keep abstaining ... from blood"
(Acts 15:28, 29). With full realisation of the implications of this position
I HEREBY:

1.   *CONSENT* (subject to the *exclusion of the transfusing of blood or blood components*) to all such necessary emergency treatment including general anaesthesia and surgery as the doctors treating me may in their professional judgement deem appropriate to maintain life.

2.   *DIRECT* (a) that such consent is temporary and only effective until such time as I am conscious and sufficiently capable of discussing further proposed treatment and giving informed consent;

(b) that such consent and any subsequent consent that I may give *EXCLUDES the transfusion of blood or blood components* but includes the administration of non-blood volume expanders such as saline, dextran, Haemaccel, hetastarch and Ringer's solution.

(c) that my express refusal of blood is absolute and is not to be overridden in ANY circumstances by a purported consent of a relative or other person. Such refusal remains in force even though I may be unconscious and/or affected by medication, stroke or other condition rendering me incapable of expressing my wishes and consent to treatment options and the doctor(s) treating me consider that such refusal may be life threatening;

and   (d) that this Advice Directive shall remain in force and bind all those treating me unless and until I expressly revoke it in writing.

3. *ACCEPT* full legal responsibility for this decision and *RELEASE* all those treating me from any liability for any consequences resulting fron such exclusion.

Dated the _____ day of _____ 19 ___

Signed: _____

Witness to Signature:

Signature: _____ Relationship: _____

Signature: _____ Relationship: _____

B. CHILDREN

IDENTITY CARD

Child's Name

Parents: _____

Address

_____   _____
                                        Telephone

IMPORTANT MEDICAL INFORMATION
ON OTHER SIDE

— — — — — — — — — — — — — — — — — — — —

As holders of parental responsibility we are deeply interested in the welfare of our child
Because of our family's convictions as Jehovah's Witnesses we ***do not accept blood transfusions***. We do accept non-blood expanders and other medical treatment. We likely can provide information as to doctors who respect our religious convictions and may already have provided medical care for us.

SEE INSIDE

— — — — — — — — — — — — — — — — — — — —

Allergies: _____

Current medication: _____
_____

Medical problems: _____
_____
_____

ADVANCE MEDICAL DIRECTIVE/RELEASE
(Child)

I the undersigned   , a holder of
parental responsibility for
born the   day of   19   , being one of
Jehovah's Witnesses with firm religious convictions have resolutely
decided to obey the Bible command "Keep abstaining ... from blood"
(Acts 15:28, 29). With full realisation of the implications of this position
I HEREBY:

1.   CONSENT (subject to the *exclusion of the transfusing of blood
or blood components*) to all such necessary emergency treatment
including general anaesthesia and surgery as the doctors treating the
child may in their professional judgement deem appropriate to maintain
life.

2.   DIRECT (a) that such consent is temporary and only effective
until such time as I am contacted and am able to discuss further proposed
treatment and give informed consent;

(b) that such consent and any subsequent consent that I may give
EXCLUDES the transfusion of blood or blood components but
includes the administration of non-blood volume expanders such as
saline, dextran, Haemaccel, hetastarch and Ringer's solution;

(c) that this express refusal of blood is absolute and is not to be
overridden in ANY circumstances by a purported consent of any person
not holding parental responsibility. Such refusal remains in force even
though the doctor(s) treating the child consider that such refusal may be
life threatening;

and   (d) that this Advice Statement shall remain in force unless and
until I expressly revoke it in writing.

3.   ACCEPT full legal responsibility for this decision

Dated the _____ day of _____ 19 ____

Signed: _____

Witness to Signature:

Signature: _____ Relationship: _____

Signature: _____ Relationship: _____

Source: Watch Tower Bible and Tract Society.

Index

References are to paragraph numbers, apart from those prefixed A which refer to Part III, Appended Materials